Manifest Error

The True Story Of A Wrongful Murder Conviction

By Dewey Olson

This story is based on real events. Details imagined.

Table of Contents

Chapter 1
September 6, 1914

Herbie pulls on his homemade woolen socks, tattered hand-me-down jeans, and blue flannel shirt, before slipping on and lacing up his worn leather shoes. He stumbles downstairs for a quick sip of coffee while his ma reminds him of his duty this morning. He glances into the kitchen and sees the sheet on the floor that is covering his dead father.

Herbie steps out of the porch door and immediately starts running the almost two miles to his sister's home. He doesn't normally get up this early in the morning, but his mother told him to get dressed and run to fetch Alex, his sister's husband. It is almost five thirty on a clear, cool September Sunday. Dawn is just breaking above the wooded bluff on the Hancock side of Portage Canal.

Fifteen-year-old Herbie knows that his mother wants to see her son-in-law Alex as soon as possible, so Herbie takes a shortcut across the neighbor's property to get to Canal Road. Once he gets to the dirt road, running is easier, but he still needs to walk to catch his breath at times. His leather work shoes are not made for long-distance running. After fifteen minutes, he crests the small hill and sees the Olson farm. Less than a half mile to go.

Hilda Olson is busy going about her usual morning routine of making a breakfast of bacon, toast, and over-easy eggs for her husband. Alex, sitting at the kitchen table, has finished some of his chores in the barn and is sipping his first morning cup of coffee. Alex and Hilda, married just over nine years now, are the parents of five small children, all girls. They own a medium-sized dairy farm on Canal Road. They hear a rapping at the front door. Alex wonders who would be calling at this time of day. This is to be no ordinary Sunday.

Alex gets up and walks to the door to find Hilda's young brother, Herbie, standing on the concrete steps. He is sweating and flushed in the face.

Speaking Finnish because it's Herbie's easiest language, Alex asks, "Why are you coming 'round this time of day when you should be home doing chores? Your pa won't like this!" Alex knows all too well how upset his father-in-law, August Lahnala, can get when he thinks his boys aren't working hard enough to earn their keep.

Alex has seen firsthand how Lahnala treats his son, John, when he thinks he is shirking his chores. If Herbie had an argument with his pa about doing chores the way his brother John sometimes had, and he is coming here to hide out, Alex wants no part of it. Alex immediately learns he's making a bad assumption.

"You gotta come quick!" Herbie blurts out in Finnish. "Pa got shot dead!"

Alex steps outside to be beyond earshot of Hilda and asks, "What happened?"

"Somebody shot Pa last night. Ma told me to run and fetch you," Herbie replies.

Alex asks, "Why didn't someone get me last night?"

"The phone don't work. We were all afraid to go outside cuz we might have got shot too!" Herbie answers.

"Wait here while I get my shoes. I'll tell Hilda where I'm going."

In the kitchen, Alex tells Hilda, "Herbie is at the door because your father is sick. Your mother asked Herbie to fetch me because she said I'd know what to do."

Hilda is eight months pregnant. She and Alex had already lost one child due to premature birth. Alex tells her a fib because he doesn't want her to be needlessly upset. Alex decides he needs to confirm what Herbie told him. If it's true, he'll gently break the news to Hilda.

Alex and Herbie go outside to start the Model T Ford.

As Alex drives to the Lahnala home, he asks Herbie, "What else can you tell me about what happened last night?"

Herbie explains, "Pa went to Hermanson's store to buy a couple of things last night after dinner. He didn't get home by the time we went to bed. About ten minutes after we went upstairs to bed, Pa got home. I heard him downstairs in the kitchen. Then I heard the kitchen door open, three shots, and something heavy fell on the floor. Ma hollered, 'What in the world was that?' and everybody in the house rushed downstairs. We found Pa laying on the kitchen floor."

"Are you sure your pa is dead?" Alex asks.

Herbie responds, "Jake looked at him last night when we got to the kitchen and said he seemed alive. But after a while, he looked again and said he was dead. He covered Pa with a sheet. Jake wouldn't let anybody else look at him."

Herbie continued, "Some of us tried using the telephone last night to call you, or a doctor, for help. But the phone didn't work. Everybody was afraid to go outside. There was no moon, and it was so dark, we were all scared we might get shot. Ma said we should wait for daylight before she sent me to fetch you."

Alex and Herbie arrive at the Lahnala home to see Herbie's Ma, Greta, simply walking around outside the farmhouse with Jake, the hired man. She comes up to the car. Alex steps out and hugs her before they walk together to the farmhouse. "What happened?" he asks in Finnish.

"I heard August in the kitchen last night after he came home from Hermanson's. I guess somebody was at the kitchen door. He opened the door and was shot!" Greta explains.

As they enter the kitchen, Alex sees what he presumes to be August's body on the floor, covered by a sheet. Nobody else is in the room. He lifts the sheet from August's body to confirm he is dead then covers him again. He asks Greta if anybody had notified the sheriff yet. Greta says, "Not yet. That's why Herbie ran to get you."

Alex tries the phone to call the sheriff. "Herbie told me the phone's not working. It still isn't. I'll drive home, tell Hilda what happened, call the sheriff, then return here with Hilda. Nobody should move anything in the kitchen or the shed until after the sheriff has arrived. He'll tell you when it's okay."

Greta replies, "The older children are in the barn doing their chores. I'll keep them and Jake out of the kitchen and shed area."

As Alex drives back home, he thinks it is strange that the family doesn't show more signs of mourning over August's death. His mother-in-law, Greta, had said that her tears and those of her children were shed during the night. Alex himself is the oldest of eight children. He hopes more tears would accompany his own death if he died this way. Perhaps the way a person lived, and died, made the difference?

Alex knows that August was sometimes a hothead. It was said August could start an argument in an empty room. But Alex never thought it possible that someone would want to murder him. Yet, after August was shot, it looked like there was little mourning for him that night.

Alex was told that the entire Lahnala household had simply returned to bed. This wasn't normal. *I wonder what I'm missing?* he muses.

Alex is aware that August's children were not strangers to hard work. Hilda reinforced his beliefs by what she said about her life before she married Alex. Greta didn't complain about her life at home, but Alex is aware of the many rumors saying that August mistreated her. Alex has put some credence in the old Finnish expression, "Love is blind, but the neighbors aren't." And the neighbors talked!

Alex also learned from his wife that August's treatment of his children, and people generally, didn't endear him to them. Six children had already left home. It was said August drove them from home with his hard-nosed manner. Once you got to know him, this was a man who was difficult to like, let alone love. August was even briefly jailed because of his violence at home.

Alex is thirty-one years old, rather tall, and of medium build. He is pleasant looking and is also strong because of the farming work he has done for most of his life. He has never warmed up to his father-in-law because August liked his alcohol and tobacco. Alex, on the other hand, is a nonsmoker and teetotaler. That difference is what attracted Hilda to him. Hilda didn't want to - in fact, she decided she could not - marry a man like her father. She married Alex in 1905 when he was twenty-one and she was twenty. Hilda has long brown hair, is a diligent worker on the farm, and is slim — that is, when she's not pregnant. She has five children.

As he drives home, he wonders how best to explain to Hilda what he's learned about her father. When he arrives home, Alex finds Hilda in the kitchen. "What's wrong with Pa?" she asks.

Alex says, "Let me pour a cup of coffee and I'll explain. Let's sit down." After pouring his coffee, he wants to gently explain what has happened but there's no way to protect her from the plain truth. "Your pa went to Hermanson's store last evening and, while he was gone, the rest of the family went upstairs to bed. When he got home, somebody opened the kitchen door and shot him. The family heard the shots and went downstairs to the kitchen to see what happened. He died last night."

Alex is surprised because Hilda doesn't seem overly shocked at the news. Like Alex, she is the eldest of her siblings. Unlike Alex, who has five siblings, she has twelve. She is thirty years old and has heard whispers and accusations about her father for many years.

"Well, I didn't expect anyone to shoot him, but I can't say I'm shocked about it." Hilda says through tears. "Pa has not been a nice man in the last few years. He hardly talks to Ma or the children except to grumble about something they did wrong."

Alex is pleased that Hilda takes the news as well as she does but is surprised that news of her father's death does not produce more of a reaction from August's eldest daughter.

Alex informs Hilda, "Sheriff Cruse doesn't know what's happened yet, so I must call him." Hilda remains at the table as he walks to the telephone and calls the Houghton County Sheriff's Office. Undersheriff William Heikkila picks up the phone.

Alex says, "This is Alex Olson from Houghton Canal. My father-in-law, August Lahnala, was shot last night and is dead on the kitchen floor at his home."

Heikkila asks, "Why is the sheriff's office just being notified now — hours after the shots were fired?"

Alex explains, "The Lahnala telephone doesn't work, and everyone was afraid to leave the house last night. I just learned of his death and am calling you from my home."

Heikkila says, "I'll relay the information to Sheriff Cruse and also contact the coroner, John Eichkern. We'll head to the Lahnala farm as soon as we can."

Having neglected many of his own farm chores for the day, Alex mentally prioritizes his morning work and promises Hilda, "We'll go to your folks' home as soon as I get a couple of my morning chores done. Tell the girls we have to go back to your ma's home after I'm finished."

August Lahnala Home

Hilda rounds up their two oldest daughters, Mabel and Florence, and explains, "Your pa and I must return to Mummu's home. You'll have to complete his chores and do yours too." They're not too pleased to be enlisted to do some of their father's work. They'll also be baby-sitting three younger kids, Betty, Eleanor, and Evelyn, while their parents are gone. Hilda doesn't know how long they'd be at Lahnala's. She adds, "I'll make a lunch so you won't have to do that." An hour later, Alex comes in from the barn, cleans himself up, and he and Hilda head out for the Lahnala farm.

As soon as they get to the farm, Alex turns onto the six-hundred-foot driveway to the farmhouse. Greta sees them coming and is outside to greet Hilda with tears and hugs. "Your pa is gone!" she exclaims. They both know that August did not treat many people nicely. But they can't understand what's happened. "Who would do this to him?" Hilda asks.

Chapter 2
Recalling August's Life

Greta, Hilda, and Alex think back in time as they try to recall what's happened in August's life. They surmise that his murder surely cannot be for something August did a long time ago because "time heals all wounds". But maybe they're wrong. Perhaps August did something in the distant past that caused somebody to feel offended. Over the years, this hurt may have festered until it boiled over.

Or did something happen more recently that caused somebody to go off the deep end in a fit of rage due to a freshly triggered emotion? The family can't recall anything happening in the recent past that was so severe as to cause anyone to take such drastic action.

Generally, August was "rough" but got along with most people. Sometimes his Finnish pride got the better of him. Certainly, August was a proud Finn! He immigrated to the United States in 1880, became a naturalized citizen in 1896, and was proud to be an American. He recognized that being an American carried some responsibilities. If he thought somebody did wrong, he wasn't afraid to say so. This caused him to make some enemies. One was Jack Lacy. Shortly after his arrival in this country, August witnessed a bar fight in which Lacy stabbed a man to death. August was called as a witness in Lacy's trial. His testimony was instrumental in sending Lacy to prison.

August was the oldest child in his family. As the eldest son, his father expected him to carry much of the weight when he was growing up in Finland. August's father did not allow his son to enjoy the luxury of a pleasant childhood. August learned how to treat all his children the same way. And August developed a temper.

His temper may have been one of the main reasons he immigrated to the United States. In Finland, if a family was a farming family, it was customary to divide a farm between the boys in the family when the parents could no longer work it. As the population increased in the

1800s, however, that custom became increasingly unworkable, as the acreage for each heir became smaller with each generation. Smaller farms meant less profit and food for the family. As time passed, the time-worn tradition changed. Soon the expectation in some families was that the oldest son in the family would inherit the entire farm. As the oldest son, August fully expected to receive the entire farm. However, his father informed him that he'd receive only half the farm as his inheritance. August said if he could not have it all, he didn't want any of it. He reverted to his plan B: he said goodbye to his family in Finland and immigrated to America.

The first impression a person had of August was "shady." Black, bushy eyebrows that seemed to extend to his black, shaggy beard and mustache. He was broadly built, squat, and had large, powerful hands. He was also tightly wound. A person got the inkling that he could jump five feet straight up — except for the heavy, clomping work boots he always wore. His usual wardrobe consisted of black pants, black coat, black vest, and the ubiquitous black hat.

Even his fingernails were ringed in black. Some said he had a nice set of "pearly whites," but there were few witnesses. He rarely smiled.

Alex tells Greta, "I telephoned the sheriff's office and talked to the undersheriff, Mr. Heikkila. Heikkila, the sheriff, and others should be arriving soon." Alex spends an hour or so with the family and, after leading them in prayer, returns home to work on his remaining chores.

Before he leaves, he reminds those at the house, "Don't disturb anything in the kitchen or in the shed leading to the kitchen." Alex then leaves Greta with the rest of her family to allow them to grieve together.

At the Houghton County Sheriff's Office, Undersheriff William Heikkila briefs Sheriff James Cruse and two deputies. "August Lahnala was fatally shot last night, and it was just reported by Alex Olson because the Lahnala telephone didn't work. Other family members and the hired man were already upstairs in bed when the shooting occurred. But that's about all I know right now."

Sheriff Cruse, Heikkila, and two deputies head to the Lahnala home in the sheriff's department Model T. They discuss what might have happened as they drive.

Passing the old Atlantic Mill, about five miles later they arrive at the community of Oskar. The Lahnala home is less than a mile away.

As Heikkila drives the group to Lahnala's, Sheriff Cruse tells him to stop the car when they near the telephone pole that has the telephone tap to the Lahnala house. "Let's look at the telephone line here," he suggests.

"Oh! The wire to the farmhouse has been cut!" a deputy exclaims. Although the grass is tall, the deputy quickly discovers pliers near the base of the pole. "Sheriff, look at this," he says.

Cruse responds, "Well, that's interesting! Let's keep the pliers as evidence."

They proceed to the farmhouse, where the sheriff eyes the uncut grass. Sheriff Cruse commands his two deputies, "Closely examine the area around the house, the doors of the shed, and the shed itself." As he enters the kitchen from the shed, Cruse notices the sink and water pump under the windows, the white-painted kitchen table and six matching chairs, and the covered body. He also notes the painting of a white-haired old man praying above his soup and bread, which hangs above the table. Considering the body on the floor, he thinks the painting is out of place. Along the wall opposite the sink is the wood-fired cookstove, which is used to make the morning coffee and to chase the morning chill out of the house.

"Heikkila, please check for anything out of the ordinary," orders Cruse.

John Eichkern, the coroner, arrives at the house about ten minutes after Cruse. "Mornin', Sheriff. Nice day to meet you out here," he says sarcastically. Eichkern enters the kitchen and calls in four men to act as a coroner's jury to provide a positive identification of the body and to determine the preliminary cause of death. He then orders, "Everybody else out of the kitchen while I examine the body."

He finds August Lahnala lying on the floor on his back with a bullet wound on the right side of his chest. His face is turned toward the kitchen stove. There is some foam on his nose. His shirt is open, but there is only a little blood from the wound in his chest. Eichkern does a more thorough review of August's body before it is moved.

After ten minutes, he instructs the deputies, "Please remove the body from the kitchen and place it in the back of my car. I'll take it to town for a more detailed examination."

While Eichkern is examining the body, Sheriff Cruse and Mrs. Lahnala are talking in the living room. "I am so sorry for what's happened here," Cruse says. "Please understand that we have some questions about your husband and why someone might want to shoot him."

In broken English, Greta says, "I understand." She offers a chair for the sheriff.

Cruse sits and says, "I was told nobody wanted to leave the house last night after the shots were fired. It was dark because the sun had set, and it was so cloudy, the moon wasn't visible. I can understand why nobody wanted to leave the house."

Greta nods her agreement.

Cruse asks, "Where were your children last night?"

Greta explains who was in the house and where in the house they were located. She then adds, "Bill, John, and our daughter Alina have left home and now live near Rumley."

Cruse asks, "Where is Rumley?"

Greta says, "It's in Alger County, southeast of Marquette — about one hundred miles from here as the crow flies. John lives with Bill and his wife Hannah down there. Alina is married to William Ollie and lives nearby."

As Cruse continues with his questions, Undersheriff Heikkila has been interviewing Jake, the hired man, and the children who were at the house the previous night.

The officers' belief that August was a demanding man is reinforced by what they learn from the family. He was born in Finland in 1864, immigrated to the United States at age sixteen in 1880, and married Greta in 1884. By 1910 he had acquired land for farming, built a two-and-a-half-story farmhouse and the requisite barn and associated outbuildings, became a successful farmer, and had thirteen children. Not bad for a poor Finnish boy who came to America with little! August expected much the same effort from his family.

As the family endures the questioning, other deputies continue their investigation. They talk to several of Lahnala's neighbors, friends, and acquaintances and discover that August has had some "run-ins" with several people. Of course, Hilda didn't know about these discussions between the neighbors and law enforcement officers until the neighbors told her. Thank goodness for neighbors who talked!

In addition to farming, August was a teamster and had delivered goods to many people and businesses in the Hancock/Houghton area for several years. In a small town, a good reputation is worth its weight in gold if you're a businessman. And, for the most part, August's business reputation has been solid. He's met many people in his business.

Sheriff Cruse is aware that August had run afoul of the law, however, about eighteen months before he was murdered. He was jailed for ten days for being drunk and beating his wife. After checking with other law enforcement agencies, Cruse also learned that August was a witness in a trial that put a man, Jack Lacy, in prison several years ago. Also, not all of his business pursuits pleased the people he interacted with.

Cruse learns that August had issues with his relationships within his own family too. It was reported that he had driven his own sons, Bill and John, from home because he couldn't maintain cordial relationships with them. It's said that they couldn't wait to be old enough to get out of August's home.

The interviews with those who were in the house Saturday night take about an hour. When they are complete, Greta asks Hilda, "What must we do for a funeral?" The question seems premature to Hilda since she just learned about her father's death. But then she realizes that Greta has had several hours to absorb what's happened.

Hilda says, "I've been thinking about that. We should talk to Reverend Heideman, to see when he's available. If he's available and we can work things out with the rest of the family, next Wednesday, September 9, would be the best day."

They suggest September 9 to the other nearby family members, and they all agree that two days will allow sufficient time for family members farther away to get home if they desire. Greta looks at Hilda and says, "You certainly didn't need this now, Hilda, with a baby due any day now."

Hilda doesn't know it yet, but her life will take another turn in about two days, when she learns that her younger brother, John, will be arrested for murdering their father.

Chapter 3
The Copper Country

Summer in the Copper Country is a beautiful time of year. The area north of the Portage Canal is an island roughly forty-five miles long by fifteen miles wide. The Finns call it "Kupari Saari," which means "Copper Island" in English. The village of Houghton lies along the south shore of the canal, and Hancock is on the island, across the canal from Houghton. The bridge connecting Houghton and Hancock is the only way for horse and automobile traffic to get from the mainland to Kupari Saari.

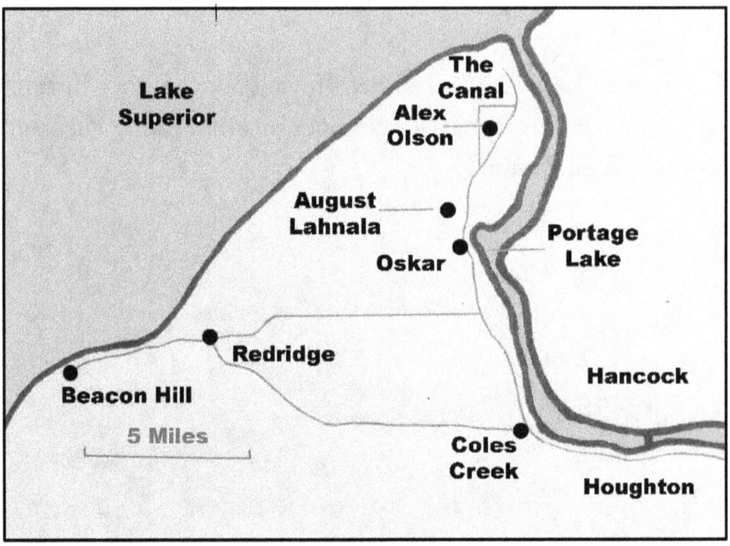

Oskar Area

The island seems like it was created by some force that lifted the area north of Houghton and moved it northward about a quarter mile. Alex liked to think that God was the force that created the island. The waters from Lake Superior flowed into the jagged edge where the earth was split by the force. This created the Portage Canal, which separated Copper Island from the mainland. Over time, erosion worked on the jagged edge. Some areas where the ground was soft eroded quickly and sloped gently to the water. The areas where the earth was rocky didn't erode as much, resulting in a much steeper slope to the water.

Geologists will tell you that this landscape was created by lava filling huge fissures in the earth. Lava flows that have captured old rocks are still evident on the north end of the island. Known as Copper Harbor Conglomerate, the rock formation is common along this section of the Lake Superior coastline.

Either creation story ultimately describes the Houghton-Hancock area. In some places, the slope is so severe that thirty feet of basement wall built into the hillside has a single cinder block exposed on the uphill end but up to eight or nine exposed on the downhill end. This slope continues for several blocks from the top of the hill toward the Portage Canal. Many streets are closed in the winter because it is dangerous for horses and automobiles to travel.

Further north on the island, the rock layers are tilted up in extreme angles, resulting in huge cliffs. Often these cliffs expose layers of minerals. In 1841, Douglas Houghton, Michigan's first state geologist, reported on the copper deposits that started the first rush of copper prospectors. This was six years before the California Gold Rush. The area became the richest copper district in the world and led the world in copper production. While copper is mined in many places in the world, Michigan copper is "native" copper, meaning it is not combined with other elements. It is pure, the color of a copper penny. At some mines, copper nuggets were found mixed with silver. Small nuggets of these "half-breeds" somehow made it into the pockets of miners as they left their places of employment. They became prized objects of discussion in the homes of the miners.

In 1845 the Cliff Mine was developed at one of the exposed cliff faces. It was the first profitable copper mine in the area, employing 840 men at its peak. At the Cliff, a horizontal shaft was dug and huge masses of native copper, from one hundred to one thousand tons, were discovered. An investment of $100,000 by the Pittsburg and Boston Mining Company provided a return of $1,269,000. Nearly forty million pounds of refined copper originated in this mine.

In 1869 the Copper Country provided more than 95 percent of the copper produced in the United States, and for thirty years after provided more than three-quarters of the nation's copper. This copper-rich area attracted miners from England, Italy, Finland, and other European countries. Up to sixty-six thousand people lived on the paychecks of a single corporation, the Calumet & Hecla Copper Company.

Some copper masses, called *float copper*, have been found just under the surface of the soil. Float copper was created by glaciers that stripped copper from its original location in prehistoric times and floated it along the surface of the earth as the glaciers moved. Pieces weighing over nine thousand pounds are on display in the Copper Country. It is an interesting place to live!

Alex loves this area, which reminds him of Finland. He is straightlaced, industrious, and hard working. He immigrated to the United States from Finland with his parents, arriving in 1889 when he was five years old. In Finland, his father was in the tar-making business. Tar was necessary for sealing the hulls of ships in the shipbuilding industry of the 1800s. His Finnish last name was Tervaniemi, which means *tar point* in English. The family farm in Finland was on the shore of a point or peninsula which, by means of rivers and lakes, eventually connected to the shipyards on the Finnish seacoast. Tar was made on the farm from the pine and birch forests in the area and transported by water to the shipyards.

Alex's family left Finland because it was under Russian control. Finland was formerly part of Sweden but, after Sweden/Finland lost a war with Russia, Finland became a Russian grand duchy. As such, it was able to keep intact its individual rights, traditions, laws, and constitution. But the Russian czar ruled Finland, and young Finnish men were conscripted into the Russian Army. Alex's father couldn't bear to see any of his children in that army.

Finnish nationalism was also on the rise in the 1800's. Finnish feelings could be summed up as follows: "We are no longer Swedes; we cannot become Russians; we must be Finns!" That attitude gave rise to a term that has been used to characterize a Finn: *sisu.* Sisu is difficult to describe. There is no literal English parallel. It stands for a cluster of traits including pride, hardiness, grit, guts, willpower, tenacity, and resilience. That's the type of attitude necessary to leave your home and settle in a new land. And that's what many Finns did.

Throughout Alex's life, late summer was his favorite season. The summer heat was pretty much gone, autumn promised cooler temperatures, haying is coming to an end, and his daily workload was decreasing.

However, this year, things will be different. His young brother-in-law and good friend, John, will need his help. Alex will do what he can to help John!

When his chores are done, Alex goes back to Hilda's family home to get Hilda. She bids her mother farewell and, on their drive back home, Alex says, "Tomorrow I'll run to town to send a telegraph to Bill, John, and Alina, to let them know what's happened."

"They'll sure be surprised!" replied Hilda.

Chapter 4
Brothers in Alger County

Bill Lahnala wakes early as his wife, Hannah, is getting out of bed. It had been a warm September night, so the fire didn't need overnight stoking. He gets the fire going in the kitchen stove and makes a pot of coffee as Hannah prepares eggs for breakfast. He and his brother John are going to look for work this morning.

John is still sleeping when Bill nudges him awake. "Is it time to get up already?" John asks in Finnish.

"Sure is, brother!" replies Bill. "Time to get rolling and find some work."

Bill and John plan to go to Gwinn and look for jobs because it is a larger village than Rumley, and job prospects are better. After breakfast, they leave Hannah with the children to catch the train to Gwinn. In Gwinn, they ask about employment at Donaldson's Hardware but don't have any luck. They try a nearby food store, but they aren't hiring. They hear that two nearby iron mines might be hiring, but they don't get any job offers from them either.

"I'm pretty discouraged," Bill says as they walk toward Little Lake. "How am I supposed to take care of my family if nobody is hiring?"

John understands his concern. "Compared to you, I don't have much to worry about. I'm just a single guy," he says. Privately, he wonders if he made a mistake when he left the Copper Country to find work near his brother.

It is late afternoon when they arrive at Little Lake. They take the train back to Bill's place for the night. They'll try to find a job again tomorrow, September 3.

When they wake up the next morning, they check at a couple of nearby lumber camps but don't get any work offers from them.

Bill says, "I've got to do some work on the house before the weather gets cold. I think I'll head home to get something done today."

John replies, "I've been wondering if anybody is hiring in Dorsey or Little Lake, so I think I'll head that way. If I get work, at least I'll be able to help keep food on your table."

When John gets to Dorsey, he stops at the train depot to rest and to get some water. While he is sitting, he's approached by the railroad section boss, Charles Lindeman, who asks what John is doing. John explains that he's looking for a job.

Lindeman asks, "Would you like to work for me on the railroad?"

John eagerly replies, "Yes!"

Lindeman says, "All right! Well, let's get moving." John follows him, and Lindeman takes him to a nearby saloon. They spend a little time there getting to know each other, then go to Lindeman's house in Old Swanzy, where Charles introduces John to his wife.

After some pleasantries, she asks, "Do you have a place for the night, John?"

"At my brother's house near Rumley, I do." replies John.

Charles says, "Why not spend the night here? That way we can get an early start tomorrow."

"That's fine with me," John replies. He spends the night at the section man's house.

The following morning, September 4, John has breakfast with the Lindeman family. After breakfast, Charles and John leave for Princeton with two other workers. When they get to Princeton, they go into a blind pig and buy some beer. After drinking a couple of beers, they leave and go to a saloon in New Swanzy. Two hours later, Lindeman says, "My wife said she'd make a light lunch for us. Let's head back to my place for a bite to eat."

John doesn't feel well after the meal. He leaves the others and starts walking to Little Lake. Feeling drowsy, he decides to take a nap in a field. It is dark when he wakes up. He has a bottle of whiskey with him, so he drinks the rest of the bottle and sleeps until about 6 a.m. on Saturday, September 5. He continues to walk to Little Lake, arriving at about 7 a.m. He goes into a saloon for a couple of drinks but still isn't feeling well. He leaves the saloon and goes into some jack pines behind a sawmill where he stays until about noon.

John gets hungry, so he goes to a store to buy some sardines and crackers for lunch. He walks back to the jack pines again to eat. At about 4 p.m., he goes back to the saloon, has a glass of beer, and walks to the train depot. He takes the train to Rumley, gets off at Ferguson, and walks to his brother Bill's house. He arrives around 8:30 p.m. and spends the night.

At breakfast on Sunday, September 6, John and Bill are talking. John tells Bill he got a job on the railroad section on Friday, but he's not comfortable with it.

"That would be good, steady, year-round work," says Bill.

John replies, "It may be. But I only worked there for a day. In that time, the section boss and I hit two saloons and a blind pig. I don't think I want to drink that much. And getting paid to drink is not honest work. I wasn't brought up that way!"

Bill nods, saying, "I can understand that."

John thinks more about it and says, "I'm not going back to the railroad. It's not a good fit for me."

Bill agrees. "Let's go into the woods. Maybe we can bag a buck."

"That sounds like a good idea. I wonder if William would like to go?"

Bill and John hike the quarter mile or so to Ollie's place and knock on the door before entering. They see their sister, Alina, and say, "Good morning!" Her husband William is already working on the walls of the house.

Bill asks him, "Would you like to hunt for a few hours?"

"I'd like to do that, but I need to cut tar paper and chink the walls of this place before the weather gets cold. I think I'll have to pass. But thanks for thinking of me!"

Bill and John go into the woods around 8 a.m. and hunt until about noon. They go back to Ollie's house and eat lunch. After eating, they take a sack into the bush to get some moss for Ollie's chinking. After about two hours, they bring the full sack back to Ollie's house.

Alina says, "Thanks, guys! This will be a big time-saver for William."

The brothers then go to Bill's house, chat for a while, and go hunting again.

John hears a shot, and Bill hollers, "I got 'im!"

John yells, "Good shootin', brother!"

They drag the deer to Bill's, cut it up, put the meat into a barrel, and get a good night's sleep after a successful hunt.

On September 7, the brothers still need to find jobs, so they both walk to a lumber camp to look for work. They are gone until about 7 p.m., and when they get back to Bill's, there is a telegram stuck in his door. Bill opens it and reads that August has been killed. He exclaims, "John, Father is dead! He was shot!"

John says, "Let me see that!" He can't read much English, but he can read enough to understand that August has been killed. They talk about his death and wonder what happened. They decide to go to Ollie's house to tell them the news. They stay at Ollie's about half an hour; tears are shed, and plans are made to travel to Houghton to be with the family and to attend the funeral. John and Bill return to Bill's place for the night.

Bill and John get up early the next morning to return to the Ollie house. About six in the morning, John, Bill and his wife, Hannah, and their children, and Alina leave for the funeral in the Copper Country.

After catching Tuesday's train in Rumley and settling into their seats, they enjoy the early fall color change of a few of the trees. Bill says, "Those trees must be sick because they're changing into fall colors too early." But they've seen early color changes in past years. Perhaps it's due to wet or cold fall weather. This isn't anything new.

Under a bright blue sky, John imagines the brook trout in the small, rippling streams they pass. The guys also think about the upcoming deer hunt and the antlers they already have hanging on their walls from past seasons.

Normally, taking a train ride would be an entirely pleasant experience, but this one is decidedly not so. Arriving in Marquette, they must switch trains to get to Houghton. Their new train is waiting for them.

By coincidence, Houghton County Sheriff's Deputy Lucas was heading to Rumley to question Bill and John Lahnala. He took Monday's train to Marquette and spent the night there. He is in the Marquette train depot on Tuesday, waiting for the train from Rumley, planning to take the train to Rumley on its return trip.

As the train from Rumley pulls into the station, passengers are talking as they depart. Lucas overhears someone say, "Bad timing for the old man to get shot now. I have a lot of work to get done on the house before winter sets in."

That prompts Lucas to say, "Excuse me. I overheard you say someone was shot. Where did that happen?"

Bill replies, "In Houghton. We're headed there for the funeral."

Lucas quickly realizes that the discussion is about the Lahnala murder case which he's investigating. He immediately changes his train ticket to return to Houghton. He rejoins Bill, John, and the rest of the family as they board the train just leaving for Houghton.

Lucas asks, "Are you the Lahnala boys?"

"Yes. I'm Bill, and he's John."

After some small talk, Lucas asks John, "Did you get along well with your father?"

"We've had our issues over the years, and we sometimes don't see eye to eye. But he is my father, and I respect that."

Lucas's impression of John is that he is modest, honest, and hard-working. His body is not as broad as his pa's. Instead, it has the chiseled look of an eighteen-year-old young man, which exudes youth and stamina. He is fair-haired, pleasant looking, clean shaven, and has bright blue eyes. Physically, he is almost the complete opposite of his father. He is also easy to talk to — if you speak Finnish. He can understand English but cannot speak it well.

Lucas says, "I'm Houghton County Sheriff's Deputy William Lucas. John, when we get to Houghton, I'd like you to come with me to the sheriff's office to answer some questions about the murder of your father."

John looks at Lucas and replies in broken English, "Well, we can do that, but I don't know anything about it. I was in Rumley when I heard it happened."

"Just the same," says Lucas, "I'd like to know more about you and your father."

John's brother, Bill, and his wife Hannah, and his sister Alina couldn't understand what Lucas could learn from John. They know that John was in the Rumley area when August was killed.

"Are you arresting John?" asked Bill.

"I reckon I am," replies Lucas.

Chapter 5
John Arrested

Upon arriving in Houghton, Deputy Lucas escorts John to the county jail. When the rest of the travelers arrive at the Lahnala home, they explain to their mother what happened. Bill says, "John was arrested! He was taken to jail when the train got to Houghton. But he couldn't have done it because he was in Rumley with us on Saturday night when Pa was killed. There must be some mistake!"

Greta asks Bill to immediately visit Alex and Hilda to tell them what happened to John. When Hilda hears that John was arrested for the murder, she is dumbfounded. She and Alex know that John couldn't possibly have done it. Of course he didn't do it! He simply is not the type of man to commit murder — especially the murder of his father. Plus, John was about a hundred miles away from Oskar the night of the murder.

Alex decides that he must go to Houghton and talk to the sheriff. He wants to hear for himself what happened. Alex immediately calls Sheriff Cruse and sets up an appointment for the next afternoon. Alex tells Cruse that Lucas must also be there.

After lunch the next day, Alex drives to Houghton and notices the early autumn colors on the Hancock side of the Portage Canal. He passes the old mill at Cole's Creek, where copper-bearing rock is pummeled by huge mill hammers to separate the rock from the copper ore. The waste rock, called stampsand, is then sluiced into nearby Portage Canal. The federal government caused the mill to close temporarily about ten years earlier because the stampsand threatened to block the canal. Secretly, Alex doesn't like to see thousands of tons of this processed rock dumped as coarse sand into the pristine waters. But this area depends on the copper mining industry. Alex knows not to get too vocal about it.

After another half mile along the Portage Canal on his left is the Bosch brewery, followed by the Van Orden coal dock, and the railroad roundhouse. The road traverses a huge hill along the canal for the last half of the route from Oskar to Houghton. Alex passes the Houghton-Hancock swing bridge, drives two more blocks, and turns right for a block through a residential area, up the steep hill to the sheriff's office. Alex wonders why anyone would want to live on such a steep hill.

Alex gets out of the car loaded for bear. As he enters the county sheriff's office building and jail, he is directed to a conference room where he meets with Deputy Lucas and Sheriff Cruse. He is offered a chair, but there aren't many pleasantries as Alex sits and brusquely asks, "What happened with John Lahnala yesterday when the train from Marquette arrived in Houghton?"

Lucas replies, "Actually, it started earlier. I was on the train with John and Bill and talked to them about their father's shooting. It appeared to me that John hated his father. My training and experience tell me that most stabbings and shootings involve one family member against another. Therefore, I arrested John on the train. When we got to Houghton, I took him to jail."

Alex says, "So, your understanding of the relationship between John and his father was why you arrested him?"

Lucas responds, "That's pretty much it. John didn't say much on the train, and I got the impression he was hiding something."

Alex says, "John was coming home to his father's funeral. Could that be why he was quiet on the train? You have no evidence against John except your gut feeling and what's happened in other cases you're familiar with? Are you kidding me?"

Lucas and Cruse offer no response. Alex rapid-fires some more questions, and Sheriff Cruse says, "I'm sorry but we can't discuss this any further because the investigation is still underway." Cruse leaves the room and Lucas follows.

Alex gets the distinct impression that the sheriff's office will not be admitting their mistake of arresting John. Alex is burning with indignation. He slowly rises and walks out of the conference room. He sees the sheriff as he leaves the conference room. He gets the sheriff's promise to call him if John is released from jail. Alex also decides to fully support John — not only with his time and effort but also financially. He knows Hilda will agree. He also knows John is innocent of this charge.

Since Alex is near the jail, he also visits John. Alex enters the jail and asks the turnkey, "May I sit with John in his cell for a few minutes?"

The turnkey knows Alex and says, "I probably shouldn't do this, but I think I can trust you. I'll give you ten minutes." He unlocks John's cell, Alex enters, and the turnkey locks the cell door, turns, and leaves.

John says, "Alex, I appreciate you coming to see me. Can you believe this?"

"No, I can't. I know you're innocent, and your family knows it too!"

Alex describes the meeting he just had with Cruse and Lucas. John understands what's happening but doesn't believe it. Knowing Alex as well as he does, John gets tears in his eyes and cannot speak. Alex understands. Emotions are raw right now. Alex says, "We should be able to get you out of here before too long. You have our full support, of course." The turnkey comes back, and Alex must leave. He gives John a brotherly hug before he says, "I'll talk to you soon," as he walks out of the cell.

As he travels back to Oskar, Alex thinks the family should wait for two days for the sheriff's office to realize their mistake. If they don't get a phone call, he will call the sheriff.

Three days later, there is no word from the sheriff's office, so Alex makes the call. Sheriff Cruse says, "We have witness evidence that John was in the Houghton area around the time of the murder. Based on that evidence, I'm sorry, Alex, but we cannot release John at this time." Cruse then ends the call.

Alex tells Hilda, then adds, "The sheriff says they got witnesses saying John was in the area when your pa was killed so they're not going to release John.

"I've been thinking. Nobody else in your family can even consider paying for a lawyer. I guess it's up to us to hire one to defend John. Financially, we're in a better position to hire one than anyone else in the family. An option would be for your brothers and sisters to pool their resources to help pay for John's legal defense."

Hilda replies, "I agree. I'm not too confident that my family can help much — but it's worth asking. Do you have any ideas who would be a good lawyer?"

"I'll ask around. Most of the people I know only use lawyers for buying and selling property, making wills, and things like that. We need a good criminal lawyer. I suppose I could ask Jeff Morrow, the lawyer we used when we bought our last forty acres. He may have a recommendation."

Alex calls Morrow, who says, "Sorry, I cannot give you any promising ideas. I've heard both good and bad about the criminal lawyers in the area. I suggest you talk to the Michigan Bar Association. They should be able to give you some ideas."

Alex thinks, *You lawyers sure stick together!* but simply replies, "I understand. I'll call the Bar Association to see what they say. Thank you, Jeff."

He next calls the State Bar of Michigan and is referred to the father-and-son law firm of Burritt & Burritt in Hancock. After more questioning, he learns about recent legal cases where Burritt & Burritt have been involved.

Alex makes some phone calls, and his confidence grows as he learns that they have a good reputation as criminal defense lawyers. He discusses hiring them with Hilda. "Burritt & Burritt have an office in Hancock. We should meet with them to get to know them and see if they're available to take the case."

Hilda agrees. "That's a good idea! We're likely going to spend a considerable amount of money, and we should try to ensure, as much as possible, that we're getting the best legal team for John. If we don't feel good about them after the meeting, we can look for somebody else."

Alex says, "I also want to get to know them better. I'm wondering about their legal strategy, how the father and son work together, what cases have they had which are similar to John's case, and other pertinent things. I'll ask if we can have a dinner meeting with them and see if they can reserve a private room. We need to discuss details."

On September 9, the local newspaper carried this story:

The Daily Mining Gazette

Wednesday, September 9, 1914

John Lahnala, Son of Murder Victim, Held on Suspicion

Youth is Arrested in Connection with Shooting of His Father at Oskar Saturday Crime Carefully Planned

Answering Knock at Door, Oskar Farmer is Killed by Three Bullets Fired from Darkness

Telephone Wires Had Been Cut to Delay Communication with Sheriff's Office

Son's Statement in Jail is Withheld by the Sheriff

John Lahnala, 18 years of age, son of August Lahnala, the Oskar farmer who was murdered Saturday night, was yesterday arrested on suspicion of being the murderer. The alleged patricide was brought back to Houghton last night by Deputy Sheriff Lucas, who made the arrest.

Sheriff Cruse would not last night give out much information about the case. He simply said that Lahnala had been arrested on suspicion of having killed his father.

He explained, however, that witnesses appeared who claimed to have seen John Lahnala in the area on the day of the murder, which was in itself a suspicious circumstance because he was believed to be at Rumley with a married brother.

Story of the Killing

August Lahnala, 53 years of age, a well-to-do Finnish farmer, living about a mile west of Oskar on the Houghton Canal Road, answered a rap on the door of his home at 8 o'clock Saturday night. As he opened the door three shots were fired from the darkness. Lahnala dropped dead inside the doorway.

Mrs. Lahnala, six children, and a farm hand were in the home at the time. They did not see the shooting, but they heard the three shots and by the time they reached Lahnala he was dead.

The explanation of Mrs. Lahnala and the others for not giving the alarm immediately was that the phone didn't work and they were afraid to go out of the house, thinking the murderer might shoot them.

When day dawned one of the people of the house gave the alarm to the neighbors. It was found the telephone wires into Houghton had been cut at a point near the Lahnala home, undoubtedly by the murderer and with the intention of shutting off immediate communication with Sheriff Cruse. A pair of wire cutters was found near the telephone pole that had been climbed for the purpose of cutting the wires. Three empty automatic pistol shells were found outside the door.

Suspicion Turns on the Son

These were all the traces from which Sheriff Cruse and his aides could build up a theory of the identity of the murderer. There seemed to be no motive. Lahnala was a peaceable man and was thought to have no enemies.

But in the investigation, it was learned that he had a reputation for not paying his farm workers promptly and that he had a reputation for being harsh with his children.

Lahnala was the father of 12 children. Six of them live away from home, some of these being married. The younger six live at home.

The officers finally ran into witnesses who claimed to have seen John Lahnala near Oskar the day of the shooting. He was supposed to be at Rumley with his brother. Deputy Sheriff Lucas was sent for him and last night Lahnala was locked up in the Houghton County jail on suspicion of being the murderer.

Sheriff Cruse would not last night give out anything of Lahnala's story. The youth made a statement, but the sheriff would not make it public, nor would he say whether the suspect denied or affirmed the charge of murdering his father.

Chapter 6
Meeting the Burritts

Two weeks after John's arrest, Alex and Hilda have a 6:00 p.m. dinner appointment with the Burritts at the Douglas House Restaurant in Houghton. Alex and Hilda arrive first, about ten minutes early.

"We've seen the Douglas House for many years but have never been inside. I'm impressed! Why haven't you taken me here to dinner before this?" Hilda asks Alex with a wink.

"Because we're conservative farmers." Alex replies with a smile and gives Hilda a hug.

Alex sees the concierge, gives him his name, and asks where they'll be meeting with the Burritt team.

"Right this way, please." he replies and leads them to a private room on the second floor.

As they enter the room, Alex notes that there are four place settings for dinner, but the table is large enough for six chairs. The room is handsomely appointed — velvety decorated wallpaper, dark oak trim and bookcases, and paintings on the walls that remind Alex of old Europe. He is impressed by what he sees.

He tells Hilda, "I'm glad the Burritts are paying for this meal. Although, I'm sure we'll end up paying for it if we hire them!"

She smiles.

Just before 6:00 p.m., William and Barney Burritt arrive. William introduces himself and his son, Barney, and encourages Alex and Hilda to be seated. There is a pitcher of ice water on the table and Barney pours them each a glass.

William opens the discussion. "I understand, Mrs. Olson, that your father was recently murdered and your younger brother, John, has been arrested for the murder. I apologize to you both for using terms like *murder*, which might be upsetting. However, I've learned that use of direct terms is important to ensure that there is no misunderstanding of what we're talking about."

Hilda replies, "Please call me Hilda. I understand why you choose the language you do. And what you shared about John is accurate. Thank you for agreeing to meet with us privately."

William asks, "Can you share with us the kind of relationship John had with his father?"

Hilda replies, "It was not a loving relationship. They put up with each other, and John helped around the family farm when he was available. If John knew what had to be done, he did it. Interactions between John and his father, however, were strained."

William understands. "That's often the case between a father and son. Sons often have better relationships with their mothers, just as daughters often have better relationships with their fathers."

Hilda continues, "It might be of more interest to you to know more about the relationship his father had with other people."

"I do want to get into that." William interrupts. "If you want to get into that now, please go ahead."

"My father was a hard man, and he didn't get along well with many people. It would be difficult to find a dozen people who would call him a 'nice guy.' He wasn't empathetic, and he didn't value relationships with people. That was true at home with his own family and with most other people he knew. He was a hard worker and expected others who worked with him to work as hard as he did."

William replies, "Barney and I have had some time to talk to a few of August's neighbors and others who knew him, and that's also the feeling we got from them. Some of the people weren't as kind in their description of your father as you have been."

"That doesn't surprise me." Hilda says.

Barney tells Alex and Hilda that he and his father had a brief meeting with John at the jail that morning. They wanted to meet John and ask him a few questions just to get to know him a little, and to judge what kind of initial impression he might make on a jury.

Alex is interested in the Burritt & Burritt law firm and interjects, "Please let us know more about your law practice."

William responds, "As you know, Burritt & Burritt is based in Hancock. I was admitted to the Michigan Bar in 1884, about thirty years ago, and practiced law in the lower peninsula in Clinton County, Clare County, and Saginaw County. My next move was to Hammond, Indiana, and I practiced there until I set up my practice in Hancock."

Barney says, "Father got me interested in the legal system as a young man. I admired what he'd been able to do for people, and I went to law school because I wanted to do what I could to help people who were in trouble. I was admitted to the Michigan Bar in 1904, and Father and I have been partners since."

William continues, "If you check further, I think you'll find that we are one of the strongest criminal law firms in this part of the state of Michigan."

Alex asks for specifics of some of the legal cases they've handled, and William relates a few of their recent cases, the basics of the legal issues, and the verdicts in those cases. Alex is impressed.

Alex says, "Hilda and I would like you to understand that, if we hire you, I will be the intermediary between you and the rest of the family. We would like to ask you to involve me in significant discussions you have with John and others. I will try to make myself available at any meetings and interviews you have with potential witnesses. I promise not to get in your way."

After a brief discussion about Alex's term "significant," the Burritts excuse themselves from the room for a moment for a private discussion. William expresses some concern about this proposed arrangement, but Barney explains, "I agree, but Alex seems very businesslike. Having lived in the area his entire life and knowing the people involved, he also knows more about the background of the people involved in this case than we'll be able to learn over the next several months." William sees Barney's point and can't disagree.

When they come back into the room, William says, "We agree with that stipulation. However, we also have a condition: if your involvement, Alex, impacts our efforts, we will ask you to excuse yourself from future meetings and involvement."

Alex looks at Hilda, who nods in agreement, and Alex says, "We agree."

William and Barney both smile and express their appreciation for the confidence being placed in their firm. William asks Barney to let the wait staff know that they are ready for the meal.

The dinner meeting lasts nearly two hours. The food is excellent, and William orders wine with his meal. Son Barney and the Olsons only drink water.

After meeting with the father-and-son team and discussing contract terms, Alex and Hilda drive the ten miles home. On the drive, Alex tells Hilda, "Burritt & Burritt have a good reputation, and I'm told the father especially has a sharp legal mind. If we hire them, we'll be getting two lawyers who will be able to bounce ideas off each other. And a jury might be sympathetic to their side because Burritt Sr. has a gimpy foot."

Hilda isn't as impressed. William Burritt will be the leading defense lawyer and does not project a strong physical presence. He is rotund — the product of a diet based on donuts for breakfast, fatty restaurant food for lunch, and too much beer at night. This inevitably caused a serious case of diabetes, under treatment now for six years, leading to a crippling foot problem which would become more of an issue in two years. His son, Barney, is taller and leaner than his father and has apparently learned that diet impacts health.

Alex says, "I'm impressed by their knowledge of John's case, their belief in John's innocence, and their eagerness to pursue justice. They've already talked to some of the people involved! Burritt & Burritt believe that they'll have the necessary time to mount a defense which a jury will believe, and which will lead to John's freedom. I especially liked William Burritt's statement, 'I will not waste my energy where it won't do much good. My energy will go to the heart of the matter.'"

Hilda respects her husband's opinion. After more discussion and consideration, she agrees. They will hire Burritt & Burritt to defend John. They also plan to discuss their decision with other family members in the next day or so.

The following day, Alex and Hilda visit John in the Houghton County Jail to tell him of their decision and let him know that Burritt & Burritt want to talk to him about the details of the situation. They tell John that Burritt & Burritt is in charge but Alex will be present whenever he's available, so he can keep the family informed. John is pleased that Alex will often be present.

Burritt & Burritt schedules a detailed interview with John for the following morning. Alex is there. The attorneys did not want to delay their interview with John because they didn't know for sure where it would lead. It likely meant time spent traveling to the Rumley area to interview potential witnesses, and it surely meant discussions with many people in the Houghton area for the same reason.

But it starts with an interview with John Lahnala, in which William Burritt asks John, "John, please tell us where you were on Saturday, September 5."

"I was in Rumley." His reply leads to two more hours of questions and discussion between John and the Burritts. After a break for lunch, the discussion continues for another two hours. Alex is tired after the meeting. But after the initial meeting with Burritt & Burritt, he feels the follow-up meetings will be much shorter and will focus on specific details of the case.

Alex feels comfortable with the questions and John's replies, but he doesn't look forward to the long discussion with Hilda when he returns home that evening. He knows she deserves to know how the Burritt team performed.

Alex also knows that he won't be able to give Hilda an adequate report and also get a good night's sleep. When he gets home, Hilda asks, "How did it go today?"

"Burritt & Burritt asked many questions about where John was on Saturday, who he was with, what he was doing, places he visited, and so on. John replied cordially and, I hope, truthfully, and the Burritt team appeared to be satisfied with his answers."

Naturally, Hilda asks for more and more details until Alex could hardly keep his eyes open. Finally, Hilda says, "It's time for sleep."

More meetings between John and Burritt & Burritt follow, and Alex attends most of them. Alex feels that the meetings are mainly for the legal team and John to get more comfortable with each other. Alex keeps Hilda apprised of the subject matter of the meetings, but little is discussed beyond what they already knew from other family members or John.

On November 6, 1914, Alex receives a phone call from Burritt & Burritt, who tell him Judge O'Brien, the Houghton County Circuit Court judge, has surprised them by agreeing to allow bail! Alex is also surprised because bail is not usually allowed in a murder case, due to the severity of the crime. But in this case, John could be freed, at least temporarily.

Alex meets with Hilda and expresses his surprise — and concern. She is delighted that John can be bailed out of jail. Until Alex says the bail amount — ten thousand dollars! Hilda wonders what this means, in more practical terms, and says, "That sounds like a lot of money."

Alex says, "It surely is. In 1891, when your father purchased the initial 120 acres for his farm, do you know how much he paid?"

"Not really. I have never given it much thought, and my parents rarely discussed money matters with me."

"He paid four hundred dollars," Alex explains. "Considering inflation, ten thousand dollars would probably buy around two thousand acres today. That's a lot of land."

"What are you telling me, Alex? It doesn't sound like we can possibly pay John's bail."

"That's exactly what I'm thinking. Do we agree, then?"

After a little more discussion, Hilda agrees. "Yes. I'm sure John would never do anything to leave us in the lurch, but …"

"I think we should meet with your mother and explain what we're thinking," Alex suggests.

Alex and Hilda meet with Greta that afternoon and explain, "Hilda and I would like to get John out of jail. And the judge granted bail. But bail for a person charged with murder is not often granted, and when it is, the price is high. In John's case, the judge set bail at ten thousand dollars. Please understand, Hilda and I cannot afford to pay for the legal team and also pay ten thousand dollars for John's bail. It's just too much for us, or the entire family, to raise."

Greta considers what Alex has said and agrees. She adds, "You're doing more than enough as things stand now — and I cannot afford it. John will just have to stay put."

Greta privately wonders what she can do to help John, and the family, pay for John's legal fees. She's been the one to hold her family together since shortly after she married August thirty years ago. As time has gone by, increased responsibility has landed on her shoulders as August has become more of a stranger.

She doesn't think it should be the responsibility of John and his siblings to fight this fight. Greta realizes that her children are at a critical time in building their lives and financial futures. If the bill for John's legal defense is split between her children, they'll all be financially hurt at a time when they cannot afford it.

Greta, however, is fifty years old and is now the sole owner of the farm she and August built together. She decides that she will investigate options which might be available to her.

On her next visit to town, she plans to talk to a financial advisor at her bank. Greta enlists the help of her daughter, Jennie. She tells Jennie, "I have a private appointment with Mr. Dubois at the bank in Houghton. I'd like you to drive me there. The meeting will take an hour or two. Please take some busy work with you to keep you occupied."

Jennie delivers Greta to the bank, and Dubois finds a vacant room for Jennie while she waits for Greta. After Greta tells Dubois of her situation, he suggests a reasonable solution: mortgage the farm. After discussing the details, she says she'd like a day to think about it. Dubois understands and agrees.

Greta remembers what it was like when she and August bought the farm. They didn't like the thought of a mortgage to pay for it. After much soul-searching, she and August agreed it was their best option. They paid off the first mortgage early. Now she decides her worry is a small price to pay to try to secure John's freedom. She calls Dubois with her decision to take out a mortgage.

The paperwork is signed three days later, and Greta informs Hilda and Alex that she has mortgaged her farm to help pay the legal fees for John's defense. They are surprised that she took this action on her own. A family meeting is scheduled to share the news with all of Greta's children.

At the family meeting, the entire family is surprised by Greta's action. One of her children is upset and says, "You have taken on a financial burden which, one way or the other, will be passed on to all of us. Simply put, the family wealth has been reduced because of John's legal fees, and now we'll all be paying."

Another of Greta's children realizes, however, that this burden was not placed on the family's shoulders by John. "John is innocent, but it will cost money to fight the legal fight. I think mother is correct and all of the family should pay. Any of us could be put in a comparable situation, and I would hope that we would support each other." After more discussion, the children agree that Greta's action was appropriate.

They also agree that they cannot afford John's bail.

Greta asks Alex to place a call to William Burritt regarding John's bail on behalf of the family.

Alex calls the Burritt Law Office and tells Jenny, their legal secretary, why he's calling. She asks Alex to hold while she calls for William. William comes to the phone, and Alex tells him, "We'd love to get John out of jail, but the family doesn't have the money for bail."

William says, "We're not at all surprised. Rest assured that things are not slowing down in our efforts. Either Barney or I will be traveling to the Rumley area to talk to the folks down there as soon as we can."

Alex replies, "Thank you. We appreciate your work for John."

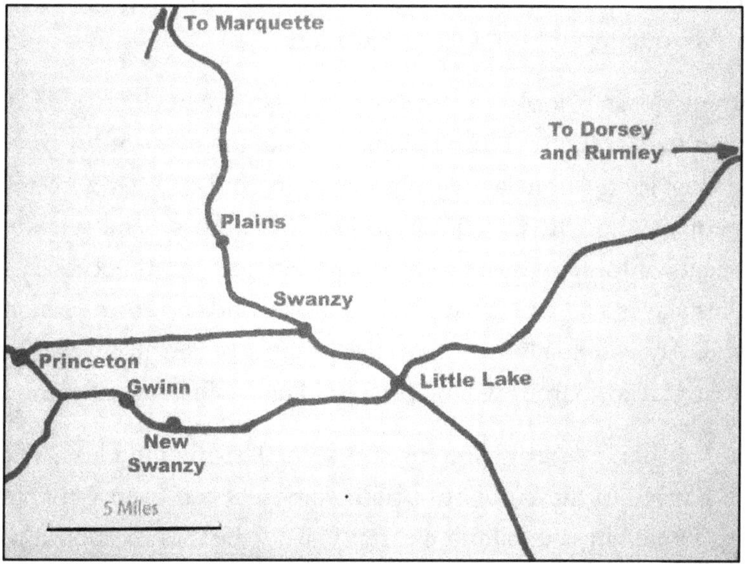

Little Lake Area

Chapter 7
Barney Goes to Rumley

During a strategy session the next day, William says, "Barney, I think it would be best if you talked to the folks in the Rumley area. My foot is acting up, and these interviews should be done soon. It's been said that 'memory diffuses fact.' We want to make sure that all of these folks confirm that John was in their area on September 5 and 6 and keep the facts straight in their minds. Maybe Jenny can make the arrangements for you. I can handle discussions with the local folks here."

Barney agrees. "That's a good plan. I'll ask Jenny to make the travel arrangements by train from Houghton to Marquette, two nights at a hotel in Marquette, and for a rental car there."

Barney doesn't look forward to the late-night train ride from Houghton to Marquette. But he plans to make the most of his travel by interviewing John Lahnala's family members and at least a couple of other people who can vouch for John. There are several who might know details of John's whereabouts in early September. If necessary, he'll extend his stay, so he won't have to make a second trip from Houghton. If they all say essentially the same thing about where John was when August was killed, Barney will be pleased. That's what he is hoping for.

On October 5, after giving his son some last-minute ideas, William delivers Barney to the Houghton train station at ten twenty-five in the evening. The night is cool and clear as Barney boards the South Shore train to Nestoria. The stars are bright, and the air is crisp. This leg of the journey should take less than two hours.

Barney finds a seat close to a heater on the second car behind the steam engine and settles in. If nothing else, at least he'll stay warm. At ten fifty-five, all passengers are on board and the train pulls out of the station. Barney is fortunate because there is nobody seated close to him.

He makes a little nest where he can relax.

Once the train is moving, he gets more comfortable. Shortly after passing through Chassell, Barney sees the Jacobsville Lighthouse at the southern entry to the Portage Canal. He is aware that there is a sandstone quarry in Jacobsville but has never been there.

Sandstone from this quarry has been shipped nationwide and was used in the Waldorf Astoria Hotel in New York City. Barney thinks that's pretty fancy for this area. He decides he must get away from work more often and see the sights in the Copper Country. Shortly after he sees the Jacobsville Lighthouse, he gets accustomed to the noises from the rails and engine and gets a little sleep.

An hour later, the train slows as it pulls into the Nestoria station, and Barney opens his eyes. It's 12:30 a.m. and Barney is tired. He must switch trains at Nestoria, so he grabs his briefcase, puts on his overcoat, and enters the Nestoria station. There is a twenty-minute layover before he can board his new train to Marquette.

Barney isn't as lucky on the second leg of his journey because there are more passengers heading to the "big city" of Marquette. He must share a seat on the right side of the train with another gentleman. They greet each other, but it's late at night, and little more is said. As they near Marquette, Barney looks out of the train window and catches sight of the rising moon reflecting off the calm surface of Lake Superior.

It seems improbable that he's been traveling nearly four hours and he is looking at the same "Super Lake" he swims in at home. Superior is huge. It is more than thirteen hundred feet deep and holds about 10 percent of the fresh surface water in the world. If it were drained, it could cover both North and South America with about a foot of water. That's big!

After leaving the train, Barney hires a car to drive him to the Windsor Hotel. He pays the driver and walks up the steps to the hotel entrance. He checks in and gets the key to his room. Finally, a bed to sleep in. He gets a short sleep, washes up, and has a hearty breakfast of eggs, bacon, and fried potatoes in the hotel dining room. He gets his rental car to drive to the Rumley/Ferguson area to meet with William Ollie. Barney had called Ollie earlier, so he is expected.

When Barney gets to Ollie's home, both William and his wife, Alina, are there. After Barney introduces himself, they all sit down and Barney asks William if he knows where John was on Sunday, September 6. Both William and Alina tell Barney that John was at their home the morning of September 6. Barney confirms that's what John has told him. Barney thanks William and Alina and asks for directions to Little Lake because he wants to talk to Bernard Goodman.

Barney finds Mr. Goodman at his store in Little Lake.

Goodman confirms that he saw John on Saturday, September 5, at the store. Goodman said he is positive because he thought John was poor and would ask for a handout after he entered the store. But John purchased crackers and sardines, and that stood out in Goodman's mind.

Barney knows that Paul Johnson works at Goodman's mill, so he asks Goodman if Johnson happens to be in the area. Goodman points and says, "Why, yes. He's working at the mill, which is just over there."

Barney asks, "Do you mind if I ask him a few questions while I'm here?"

"Not at all. Please go ahead." Goodman replies.

Barney walks to the mill, finds Johnson, and confirms that he saw John walking past the mill on September 5.

On his way back to Marquette, Barney stopped in Swanzy to interview Charles Lindeman, who confirms that he hired John on September 3 to work on the railroad line. The crew spent the night at Lindeman's house, and on September 4, they went to LaRochelle's bar. Barney gets directions to the bar, and LaRochelle also confirms that he saw Lindeman and his crew in his bar on September 4. Barney shows LaRochelle a picture of John, and LaRochelle confirms that John was part of the crew.

Barney is completely satisfied with the results of the interviews he's had and is convinced that John is telling the truth. It's been a long and fruitful day as he drives back to the Windsor Hotel in Marquette. Upon arriving there, he telephones his father with the news, and William tells him, "That's great news, son. If you're satisfied with what you've heard, come back home. I've contacted a few people in the Houghton area and have had mixed results. We can talk more about your day when you get back."

Jenny had booked Barney a room for two nights. That allows Barney to enjoy a leisurely meal that evening. He figures he deserves a reward for his work today but wonders what his father has learned, or what part of John's story he could not confirm. He spends the remainder of the evening and much of the following day on the train to Houghton, jotting notes and mentally putting together the pieces of the John Lahnala story.

When Barney arrives in Houghton, his father meets him at the station. As they drive home, Barney explains, "I've been able to corroborate essentially all of John's story."

William is pleased and jokes, "Well done. Maybe you should get more than your usual 40 percent of the corporate earnings if we win this trial."

"I'm all for that!"

William continues, "I'm afraid I haven't had such good luck."

"What's happened?"

"That's just it — nothing. I heard that a man by the name of Jacob Miller threatened August. I called Miller on the telephone, and he said he already talked to somebody called Heikkila. I figure Heikkila must be the undersheriff. But now Miller said he's sick and doesn't want to get mixed up in any legal stuff. Then he hung up."

William continues, "And there's a guy by the name of Lacy. August testified against him in a trial about twenty-five years ago. Lacy was found to be guilty, was sent to prison, served his sentence, and has been released. I tried to find him, but he seems to have vanished into thin air. So, you see, I haven't had much luck."

Barney volunteers, "Why don't I give Miller a couple of weeks to get feeling better and then I'll stop at his house. I doubt if he'll slam the door in my face."

"Won't hurt to try."

Ten days later, Barney stops at Miller's home.

Apparently, nobody is home because his knocking at the door is unanswered. "Well, if he's out and about, he must be feeling better." Barney says to himself.

Four days later, Barney calls Miller on the phone. Miller answers the call and asks, "What is this about?"

"My name is Barney Burritt, and I'm one of John Lahnala's lawyers. Do you have a few minutes to talk?"

Miller responds, "I already talked to William Heikkila. If you want to know anything, talk to him." Barney hears the click as Miller hangs up.

Barney and his father discuss Miller's refusal to talk. William suggests, "Something's not right here. Miller just isn't acting normal. I checked, and his second wife divorced him on the same grounds as his first wife: cruelty. Sounds like he's just not a very nice guy. I suppose we could talk to Heikkila to find out what he knows. I'll stop at the sheriff's office tomorrow to talk to him."

The next morning, William visits with Heikkila. Heikkila says, "Miller hasn't said much. Said he was feeling poorly for the past few weeks and was sure he was at home on September 5 because he hasn't been out often. He just seems like a crotchety old man to me. Not much different than my old man."

"Did you do any other follow-up on where he was on September 5?" asks William.

"Naw, we just chalked up his nastiness to old age and let it go."

Chapter 8
Jury Selection

On Friday, February 12, jury selection for John's trial starts. The group of twenty-four potential jurors are sworn in by Judge Patrick O'Brien. "Do you solemnly swear that you will truthfully answer all questions regarding your competency to function as jurors in this case, so help you God?" All of them mumble "I do" and take their seats.

Mr. William Galbraith makes a statement to all potential jurors stating the charges in this case. He asks, "Do you have any mental or conscientious scruples against finding any person guilty of a serious crime on circumstantial evidence?"

Judge O'Brien defines "circumstantial evidence" as a fact that is inferred from another group of facts. For example, if boot prints are seen in the snow, it can be inferred that a human made those prints.

After this explanation, potential juror number eight explains, "I'm sorry, Your Honor, but I cannot convict a person accused of a crime as serious as this one based solely on circumstantial evidence." He is dismissed.

Potential juror number fourteen is also dismissed for the same reason.

When the jurors are asked if they would convict if evidence indicated beyond a reasonable doubt that the defendant was innocent, potential juror number six asks if there is a plain definition of "beyond a reasonable doubt".

Judge O'Brien explains, "'Beyond a reasonable doubt' means that evidence and arguments which are presented are so clear that a rational person would accept them as fact. If a person cannot accept evidence or testimony as fact, they are not convinced beyond a reasonable doubt."

Number six says, "Thank you, Judge." He rubs his chin for a few seconds and confesses, "I guess I have difficulty with that concept." He is excused.

Other potential jurors are excused because they know something about the case or have some feeling about the guilt or innocence of the defendant. One potential juror requests a definition of the term "that all are presumed to be innocent." After an explanation, he is satisfied and is kept on the panel. Finally, after six hours of voir dire, a jury of twelve men and three alternate jurors is established.

It's getting late in the day, so Judge O'Brien says, "We've made good progress today, and it's getting rather late, so I think we'll adjourn until 1:00 p.m. Monday afternoon."

He cautions the members of the jury, "Do not discuss the case among yourselves or, of course, with family members or members of the public. If anyone attempts to discuss the case with you, report it to me or to Sheriff Cruse. Is that understood?"

Jury members offer the standard mumbled, "Yes, Your Honor." Judge O'Brien wishes everyone a pleasant weekend, and court is adjourned.

Chapter 9
The Trial Starts

It is Monday, February 15, 1915, and Alex and Hilda drive to the Houghton County Courthouse for the first day of John's trial. They drive past the Lahnala home and down a slight hill and over a bridge where Schlot's Creek flows into a bay on Portage Canal. The ice rink on the bay is vacant now, but evenings here at this time of year are busy with kids clearing snow off the ice to play hockey and for oldsters to enjoy skating. A small warming shack with a wood stove is on the shore of the lake, which helps keep rosy cheeks from freezing.

Alex is pleased that the road is almost snow free. Parts of the Copper Country often receive over three hundred inches of snow in a single winter season. Heavy, periodic snows occur, but conditions must be right for this "lake effect" snow to occur. Lake Superior must be relatively warm, so there's a chance for lots of evaporation, and winds must be cold and from the right direction, so the air can pick up a lot of moisture and deposit it in the form of snow on the Keweenaw Peninsula. Superior has been colder than normal, and the early winter has been cool, but not cold, so there hasn't been much evaporation from the lake. And a long, warm January thaw has melted so much snow that easy travel via automobile has been possible. A typical year would mean large horse-pulled rollers would be used to pank the snow on the roadways. That hasn't been necessary on most days so far this season.

As Alex and Hilda near the courthouse, they see the structure looming above the homes in the neighborhood. It is an imposing Victorian structure and speaks of the importance of the business for which they are there.

Hilda says, "This surely is a tall, grand building," as she and her mother accompany Alex.

Once in the building, Hilda says, "I doubt if I can attend the proceedings regularly." Looking at Alex, she says, "Your first son, Ernie, is only five months old, and we have the other children at home that all need attention." Alex understands.

A sign directs Alex and Hilda to the Circuit Courtroom on the third floor. As they walk up from the first floor, Hilda remarks, "These wide staircases and the mahogany railings are majestic!"

Alex doesn't respond but smiles and thinks, *That's my bride!*

As he enters the courtroom, Alex is struck by the small size of the room and considers the immensity of some of the legal questions which have been decided in it. Handsome, heavily varnished mahogany barriers separate the judge, the witness stand, and the legal teams from the six plain, wooden benches used by observers and potential witnesses. The overhead lights, coffered ceiling, and mullioned windows reflect softly off the polished oak floor.

Above the suppressed excitement in the courtroom, Hilda and her mother, Greta, chat about the formal look of the courtroom as they take their seats on the front bench immediately behind Barney and William Burritt's seats. Alex sits next to Hilda and is eager to see John and his legal team when they enter the room.

Houghton County Courthouse

John and the team soon enter from Alex's right. John nods and flashes a quick smile as he sees his mother, sister, and Alex. He is wearing the casual clothes Hilda brought him for the trial and is seated with his team on the left side of the courtroom. The prosecuting attorney and his associates are seated across the center aisle to the right side of the room.

Shortly after John enters, Bailiff Trudell stands and announces in a loud voice, "Hear ye. Hear ye. Hear ye."

Trudell's voice is uncharacteristically shrill and rises above the muffled chatter in the courtroom. Having secured the attention of those in the room, Trudell continues, "The Circuit Court for the County of Houghton and State of Michigan is now in session. The Honorable Patrick O'Brien presiding. All rise!"

Judge O'Brien enters and sits behind his imposing wooden desk with the American flag on the left side of the room and the Michigan state flag on the right. When he is seated, Bailiff Trudell says to those in the courtroom, "You may be seated."

O'Brien says, "Good afternoon, everybody. I am Judge Patrick O'Brien, and we are here to listen to the arguments relating to the murder of August Lahnala on September 5, 1914.

"This case might attract considerable attention because it is a murder case, and the defendant is a handsome young man. I want to remind everyone that this is a court of law. Interruptions and outbursts will not be tolerated.

"There will be members of the press in attendance in the courtroom, reporting on the events of the day. Photographs, however, will not be permitted in the courtroom. Are there any questions?"

After a brief pause, O'Brien says, "Hearing none, we will proceed."

Mr. Galbraith, attorney for the People, makes a request, "Your Honor, I ask the Court's indulgence for the People to allow a few more witnesses of which I learned last Friday."

William Burritt responds, "I object, Your Honor. The People have had adequate time to prepare for this trial. Also, the prosecution did not give notice of intention in a timely manner."

The Court replies, "The task before us is to conduct a fair and impartial trial. If an additional witness or two will help us do that, it seems to me that we should allow them to tell us what they know. The objection is overruled."

Burritt says, "Note an exception."

The Court answers, "Exception granted."

Hilda whispers to Alex, "What does 'exception' mean?"

Alex quietly replies, "Barney Burritt explained that to me earlier. He said his father knows the law better than most judges and often calls for 'exceptions.' He told me that an exception is an instance where the lawyer does not agree with the ruling of the Court. In the event of an appeal to a higher court, the higher court may determine that the original court judge did not properly apply a legal principle. And, with an eye to the future, that could be grounds for a new trial. William Burritt is a smart lawyer, and that's why we hired him!"

Hilda nods her understanding.

After these proceedings are completed, William Burritt addresses the Court. "Your Honor, the People and the Defense want to ensure that a witness's testimony isn't tainted by the testimony of earlier witnesses. We request that the Court excuse potential witnesses from the courtroom except when giving testimony. Mrs. Lahnala (John's mother), Mr. Heikkila (the Undersheriff), and Mr. Eichkern (the Coroner and Justice of the Peace) may stay. After a witness gives testimony, the defense and prosecuting attorneys agree that the witness may stay in the courtroom."

The judge says, "This is a reasonable request and is granted."

The judge starts the more formal proceedings by saying, "In this case, there are no witnesses who can state they saw who murdered Mr. Lahnala. The case of the People, therefore, is based on circumstantial evidence. The law in the state of Michigan is that, in cases of circumstantial evidence, which this case is, this Defendant is presumed to be innocent of this crime, and every man on this jury must say he is innocent until the facts presented here convince every man on this jury that he is guilty to a moral certainty. The law defines circumstantial evidence by saying that *all* evidence must point toward the guilt of the defendant, and in no other direction.

"The law requires the prosecution to prove a set of facts and circumstances, termed a chain of evidence, that points directly toward the guilt of the defendant and that are inconsistent with any other theory except the guilt of the defendant. There must be an unbroken chain of links of evidence with each one directed toward the guilt of the defendant. If one of those links should be wanting, or is not proven to a moral certainty, the entire chain fails, and the prosecution's case falls to pieces. In that event, it is your responsibility, gentlemen of the jury, to find the defendant not guilty."

O'Brien then asks, "Are the People ready to proceed?"

Mr. Galbraith, replying for the People, says, "We are, Your Honor."

The Court asks, "Is the Defense ready to proceed?"

William Burritt, principal attorney for the Defense, replies, "We are, Your Honor."

The Court says, "Your opening statement, please, Mr. Galbraith."

"Thank you, Your Honor."

Chapter 10
Prosecution Opening Statement

Mr. Galbraith starts his opening statement to the jury. "September 5, 1914, was a Saturday, and Monday, September 7 was Labor Day. In Oskar, there is a small group of houses, a little store operated by Herman Hermanson, and a creamery. There is a road on that side of the Portage Canal from Houghton to Oskar, to the farming area beyond, and to the area called 'The Canal'. Just beyond Oskar is the farm of the late August Lahnala on the left.

"On Saturday, August Lahnala and a crew were pressing or baling hay. After the Lahnala family had their supper, August went to Hermanson's store for supplies and returned home about 8 p.m. Testimony from Mrs. Lahnala, a boy, and a hired man will show they were upstairs at the home. The hired man had gone to bed, and Mrs. Lahnala and three or four children were upstairs. Mrs. Lahnala and the children heard a noise, but the hired man did not.

"One of the witnesses will say he heard three shots. Witnesses will say they heard something heavy fall. Mrs. Lahnala, the hired man, and the boy, Herbert, went down the stairs, which open to the kitchen. When they got to the kitchen, they found August lying on his back with a bullet wound in his chest, apparently dead. Somebody tried to use the telephone, but they were unable to make a call. Nothing else was done that night because occupants of the house were afraid that they might get shot if they went outside into the darkness.

"In the morning, Herbert Lahnala went to the home of Alex Olson, a brother-in-law. The sheriff and coroner were notified, went to the Lahnala home, and found Lahnala as he had fallen. In the subsequent investigation, the telephone wires at the road leading to the Lahnala farm were discovered to be cut. There is a brace pole which supports the main pole. It appears that somebody climbed the pole and slid down. A pair of pliers was found near the pole. Also, the ground near the pole was freshly plowed. A boot mark was found in the soil and was measured.

"When officers asked what happened the previous night, one of the witnesses in the house reported hearing three shots. Three shells from a Colt automatic pistol were found in the shed adjoining the kitchen.

"Further investigation revealed that there were some small children who lived at home. Three children, Bill Lahnala, John Lahnala, and Mrs. William Ollie lived near Rumley, southeast of Marquette. Inquiry showed for several years there was bad blood between August and John.

"Testimony will show that several months before the murder, John left home and worked for John Zurcher.

"Zurcher lives between Houghton and Oskar. For some of the time John worked for Zurcher, he lived with Zurcher. The rest of the time he lived with his brother who lived near Zurcher. There was a young lady working at Zurcher's who kept company with John. The Zurcher's didn't understand the Finnish language.

"The young lady overheard conversations in which John threatened his father. John showed her a Colt pistol and said, 'This is what I will kill the old man with' or words to that effect. Bill Lahnala purchased that pistol which is the same caliber as the cartridges which were found at the Lahnala house. The pistol was sold or traded to John.

"The People will show that four young people who knew John saw him make a purchase in a Houghton candy store the evening prior to the murder.

"The People will also show that Rumley is southeast of Marquette. In that area there are three railroad stops: Little Lake, Old Swanzy, and New Swanzy. There is also a branch to a place called Princeton. Testimony will show that the defendant, John Lahnala, and his brother Bill went west from Rumley on the morning of Thursday, September 3. They separated, with John going to the Little Lake station.

"It was raining when the railroad foreman came into the station. He asked John if he wanted work. John worked that afternoon and Friday morning. About noon on Friday, September 4, John left because he didn't feel well. He was seen walking northward on the railroad track. It will also be shown that it is possible to leave the Little Lake area in the afternoon, catch the train to Marquette, transfer to the South Shore train, and get to Houghton at a time earlier than when he was seen in a candy store in Houghton.

"Testimony will also show that a person could leave Houghton at 10:45 p.m. on the evening train and be in Rumley by 10 a.m. the following day. It will also show that John Lahnala was seen in Alger County on September 6, the day after the shooting.

"Now, gentlemen, the People will introduce evidence to establish the guilt of the defendant, John Lahnala, of the felonious killing of the deceased, August Lahnala. It will be your duty to take the facts as presented, to analyze them to determine the value of any testimony that may be introduced, and whether the People have, beyond a reasonable doubt, established such facts which warrant you in saying that the defendant is guilty.

"I will simply ask you to approach the case open-mindedly, without any prejudgment for, or against, any man, and to recognize and carry through every stage of this case the principle which the Court will lay down to you of the presumption of innocence.

"The subsequent happenings, and there will be many of them, will unfold themselves as the case is developed.

"Thank you."

The Court says, "Please call your first witness, Mr. Galbraith."

Chapter 11
Eichkern and Stockley Testimony

TESTIMONY OF JOHN EICHKERN

Galbraith says, "The People call John Eichkern."

After Eichkern takes the stand and is sworn to tell the truth, Galbraith requests, "Please state your name and occupation."

Eichkern replies that he is the Township Coroner and Justice of the Peace. At Galbraith's request, he then relates that he received a call from Undersheriff Heikkila on Sunday, September 6, 1914, to proceed to the August Lahnala home. He went as requested, finding the body of August Lahnala on the kitchen floor. There was a bullet hole by his right collar bone with some blood.

Galbraith thanks him, and the Court asks, "Do you have any questions, Mr. Burritt?"

William Burritt replies, "No, Your Honor."

The Court says, "Call your next witness, Mr. Galbraith."

TESTIMONY OF WILLIAM STOCKLEY

Galbraith says, "The People call William Stockley."

William Stockley is sworn, takes a seat on the witness stand, identifies himself, states that he is a civil engineer and surveyor working for Houghton County, and says he was asked to take measurements and photos of the Lahnala home. Several photos are introduced as People's exhibits. After Burritt's review, he has no objection to their being admitted as evidence.

Galbraith asks, "What does this photo purport to show?"

Stockley replies, "Photo 1 is of the Lahnala farm."

Burritt objects, "The photo itself shows what it is."

The Court says, "Overruled."

Burritt says, "Take an exception."

Galbraith asks if Stockley made any maps of the territory around Oskar. Stockley replies he did and produces a map. Galbraith asks him to describe it, and Stockley replies, "Here is Hancock, Houghton, Oskar, the Lahnala farm, and the Canal Road."

Galbraith says, "I'd like this map to be labeled People's Exhibit 4."

Burritt has no objection.

Galbraith asks, "Mr. Stockley, did you make a layout of the Lahnala kitchen?"

Stockley produces a print and points to it, saying, "I did the entire first floor of the home including the shed. The kitchen is here."

Galbraith says, "The People ask for the print of the first floor to be entered as People's Exhibit 5."

He then asks, "Please show how the kitchen contents are laid out."

Burritt objects. "Items in the room might be different than on September 5 when the murder occurred."

The Court allows the drawing and says, "Witnesses can say if the locations of any objects have changed."

Burritt notes an exception, explaining his objection to the Court. "This witness is not qualified to state where things were located the night of September 5."

Alex thinks, *I wouldn't have thought about that! Excellent point, William!*

Galbraith says, "I withdraw the question."

A point for the good team! thinks Alex.

Galbraith continues, "Please describe the layout of the shed and kitchen."

Stockley says, "The floor in the shed is one step lower than the kitchen floor. These are the door to the shed, the door into the kitchen, the kitchen window, the pantry, the stairway upstairs, the stairway to the basement, and the location of the kitchen table and cookstove."

Galbraith refers Stockley to People's Exhibit 3 and asks, "What does point C represent?"

"It's a dent in the floor."

"What about a point marked A?"

"It's a bullet hole through the door."

Burritt objects, saying, "It's just a hole through the door, isn't it?"

Stockley replies, "It's a bullet hole, Mr. Burritt."

"Did you see it get made?"

"No, but I have been examining them for about fifty years."

Burritt mutters, "All right."

Galbraith asks, "As a surveyor, have you done a lot of walking?"

"I have."

"What is the average walking rate on a good dirt road?"

Burritt objects, saying, "It's incompetent and immaterial."

The Court allows the answer, and Burritt notes another exception.

Stockley responds, "Three miles per hour is a slow pace, five miles per hour is a good one, and four is about average."

CROSS-EXAMINATION BY BURRITT

"Have you ever been in a walking race?" asks Burritt.

"I have not." replies Stockley.

Burritt says, "I believe you said the average walking speed of a man is about four miles an hour. Is that dependent on his age?"

Stockley says, "Strictly speaking, it is not. But it is dependent on his activity."

Burritt shows his sore foot and asks, "Do you think I could average four miles an hour?"

Stockley responds, "I wouldn't want to bet on it!" and the courtroom erupts in laughter.

Burritt says, "I'm done with this witness."

Chapter 12
William Heikkila Testimony

Mr. Galbraith says, "The People call William Heikkila."

"Please state your name and occupation."

Heikkila answers, "I am William Heikkila and serve as the Houghton County Undersheriff."

Galbraith asks, "Please share how you became involved in this case."

Heikkila replies, "I was called to the Lahnala home on September 6, just before 7 a.m."

"And you went to the home?"

"Yes. Sheriff Cruse, John Eichkern, and I reached the home about 8 a.m."

"And what did you discover at the Lahnala home?"

"At the road, we noticed that the telephone wires were cut. At the house, we found Mr. Lahnala lying on the floor on his back with a bullet wound on his right side. His face was turned toward the stove and there was a lot of foam on his nose. His shirt was open, but there was only a little blood from the wound in his chest."

"Did you speak to any family members?"

"I asked Mrs. Lahnala if she had any suspicion of anyone."

Burritt objects. "He is incompetent to testify what she said."

The Court agrees. "Sustained. Do not share what she said."

Galbraith says, "Please continue."

"While I questioned Mrs. Lahnala, she told the boy to go to the drawer and get three empty shells from a .32 automatic. I put them in my pocket and questioned the little boy in regard –"

Burritt objects. "I have no objection to the witness stating what he did or what he saw, but I object to any questioning of any conversation that was had at that time with the little boy or anybody else."

The Court says, "You need not state what the little boy said."

Heikkila continues. "The sheriff, Nels Burkman, Frank Eilola, and I then went out to look over the oat field there. It seemed somebody had been lying in the field close to the house. I left them there and went to the pole where the telephone wire was cut. I examined the pole very closely and could see somebody had slid down. I found a pair of pliers by the pole, so I picked them up. I examined the pole very closely again and found the party that came down the pole slid down and left a track in the dirt, freshly plowed ground. I took a measurement of that footprint with a piece of the telephone wire. By that time Peter Burkman had come over there. I showed him what I found and called the attention of the sheriff to it."

Galbraith takes a wire off the table and asks Heikkila, "Is this the wire you used?"

"It is."

Galbraith says, "I would like this wire marked as People's Exhibit 7. I ask that People's Exhibits 4, 5, 6, and 7 to be entered as evidence."

Burritt has no objection.

Holding the pliers, Galbraith asks, "Are these the pliers you found at the base of the pole?"

Heikkila replies, "Yes. I found them in a little ditch. It was a very foggy morning, so the ground was damp."

Galbraith says, "I'd like these pliers to be identified as People's Exhibit 8." Burritt has no objection.

Galbraith turns his attention to the empty shells and asks, "Mr. Heikkila, can you explain these shells?"

"They're the ones which were given to me at the farmhouse."

Galbraith asks the Court to have them marked People's Exhibit 9 and be entered in evidence. Burritt has no objection.

Galbraith asks, "When did you first see the defendant, John Lahnala?"

Heikkila says, "I first saw him on Monday, September 7, at about 8:15 p.m. at the South Shore Train Depot in Houghton. He was taken to the sheriff's office to be questioned, with Bill Lucas and Joe Wills also present.

Burritt says, "I object unless they show that the statements made by the defendant were voluntary statements, no influence of any kind brought to bear against him to make the statement."

The Court says, "I will sustain that objection."

Galbraith continues, "You have stated that you questioned him."

Heikkila says, "Yes, sir."

Galbraith says, "I will ask you whether the statements were made voluntarily on the part of John Lahnala?"

Burritt objects. "The question is leading and calls for a conclusion by the witness."

The Court sustains the objection.

Galbraith withdraws the question. He asks how John Lahnala responded to the questions asked.

Heikkila says, "He answered everything we asked him. In fact, first when we brought him into the office, his brother was there, and he also made a statement. The brothers were in different rooms when they made their statements. I wrote a memorandum of John's statement."

Galbraith says, "I'd like this to be marked People's Exhibit 10 for purposes of identification."

Heikkila continues, "John saw that his words were being recorded. I wrote some, and I had sore eyes, so Wills took over."

Galbraith requests, "Please read the statement."

Burritt immediately says, "I object because the statement hasn't been proven to be voluntary."

Galbraith asks for the jury to be briefly dismissed, and the Court dismisses them.

Galbraith says, "In the case of the People vs. Barker, the presumption is that confessions have been freely made until the contrary appears. If you, Mr. Burritt, contend that John Lahnala's statement was secured through coercion, threat, or offer of favor, it's up to you to prove it."

The judge says, "That's the way I understand the rule. If counsel wishes to do so, I shall permit him to cross-examine this witness on the competency of the confession and introduce any other evidence he chooses on that question. If there is room for different inferences, whether it is voluntary or not, it becomes a question for the jury to decide whether it was freely and voluntarily made."

The judge also says, "There is a question as to whether Mr. Heikkila can read from Lahnala's statement or simply use it to refresh his recollection."

Galbraith says, "It can go either way."

Burritt claims, "You can only use it for refreshing your recollection because the memorandum is not admissible in evidence. A witness cannot read from the notes he took. He can only use them as a memory aid. I also object to the reading of the notes because that's an indirect way to get the memorandum into evidence."

Alex is following the logic and thinks, *Lawyers can be as sneaky as anybody else. Thanks for keeping a careful eye and ear peeled, William! That's what we're paying you for.*

The Court rules, "The witness can use the statement for a memory aid and read from it as needed."

Alex thinks, *Well, that didn't go too far.*

Burritt objects. "Take an exception."

The jury is then returned to the courtroom.

Galbraith says, "Please repeat John Lahnala's statements, referencing the written memorandum as necessary."

Burritt objects. "May I ask if both the questions and the answers are in the memorandum?"

Heikkila says, "I only recorded the answers."

Burritt asks, "So, the questions ain't there?"

Heikkila replies, "That's correct."

Burritt asks, "How can the jury or anybody make any sense of the memorandum if they only hear the answers without knowing the questions?"

Agreeing, the judge says, "Mr. Burritt, your objection is sustained."

Alex smiles and thinks, *Another excellent point, William!*

Galbraith tells Heikkila, "Please refer to the statement as much as necessary and tell the jury the basic story that John Lahnala told you."

Heikkila refers to John's statement and says, "John told me he resides at Rumley. On Thursday, September 3, he and his brother Bill went to the cedar camp to look for work but didn't get any. They went back to Little Lake, where they separated. It was raining, so John went to the train depot to dry off. The railroad section boss saw him there and asked if he wanted work. John said he did and went with him to his home, where he spent the night.

The next morning, John and the section boss drove to Princeton and met another section boss. They started to drink at a saloon near New Swanzy, John got drunk, didn't feel well, went to sleep in a field, woke up at night, went back to the saloon, got drunk again, and then went home to Rumley."

Galbraith asks, "Did John Lahnala make any reference to owning a pistol?"

Heikkila replies, "Yes, sir. John told me he bought a pistol from his brother Bill when he worked at Zurcher's."

CROSS-EXAMINATION BY BURRITT

Burritt asks, "Now, Mr. Heikkila, didn't John Lahnala say to you that after they went to this saloon at New Swanzy, after they did the drinking, that they took the gasoline railroad car and went to Old Swanzy?"

Heikkila responds, "No, sir."

"He didn't tell you that?" Burritt asks.

"No, sir."

"And didn't he tell you that at noon on Friday, the fourth of September, he went and took his dinner with the section man in Old Swanzy?"

"No, sir."

"He didn't tell you that?"

"No, sir."

"Now, didn't he tell you that sometime during that afternoon that he walked down the railroad track from the Old Swanzy depot and that after he had gone down the track a little way, he laid down and went to sleep?"

"No, sir, he did not."

"Mr. Heikkila, did you take any notes of your discussion with John?"

"I only recorded the answers he gave."

"So, if you asked John a question and he didn't know the answer, what did you record?"

"I didn't write anything."

"It would have been a good idea to write the questions and the answers." suggests Burritt.

The judge says, "Enough of the comments, Mr. Burritt."

Burritt replies, "I apologize, Your Honor."

Burritt walks to the witness stand and continues questioning Heikkila. "Didn't he tell you he lay down and went to sleep and slept 'til after dark?"

"He told me after he got drunk in the saloon, he went in the field and went to sleep."

"Didn't he tell you he lay down and went to sleep and slept 'til after dark?"

"I forget. He told me he got drunk twice and went in the field twice, I understood in the morning and afternoon, and slept 'til about suppertime."

"Now, didn't he tell you that on Friday afternoon, or after he had eaten his dinner on Friday, he started down the railroad track and that he was drunk and that he laid down under a tree and went to sleep and slept 'til dark, or something to that effect?"

"He told me that in the afternoon …"

"Just answer my question."

"Yes, sir."

"And he awoke."

"Yes, sir."

"And got up and saw it was dark."

"Yes, sir."

"And he lay down and went to sleep again."

"Yes."

"And when he woke the next time, it was morning. Didn't he tell you that?"

"I can't remember that part of it."

"What?"

"I can't remember it."

Alex thinks, *I'm glad I'm not on the witness stand. Burritt is really badgering Heikkila. I'm surprised Galbraith doesn't object.*

Burritt continues his questioning. "Don't you remember that he told you he woke up, it was dark, he lay down in his nest and went to sleep again and continued to sleep until the next time he woke? It was then morning, and he got up. Do you remember? That was Saturday morning."

Heikkila says, "He said he slept in the night."

"Tell me whether you remember his stating to you that he laid 'til dark, woke up, laid down and went to sleep again, and slept 'til morning?"

"I don't remember that. He told me he went to sleep, woke up, and went home."

"Didn't you just say he told you he went to sleep, that he woke up, and laid down again?"

"I don't remember him waking up, from his statement."

"And didn't he say he laid down again?"

"He told me he went to sleep, he woke up, and went home."

"Didn't he tell you, and didn't you once state in your testimony, or did I misunderstand you, that he told you that he woke up and that it was dark, and he laid down again and went to sleep again?"

"I didn't —"

"Examine your memorandum and see if you have anything of that description there."

"No, sir, it doesn't say anything about him waking up in the night."

Burritt asks, "He simply said — he told you he lay down and went to sleep and woke up and it was dark. Is that it?"

Heikkila said, "He woke up and went home."

"Didn't he say to you that when he woke up it was dark?"

"No sir, he didn't tell me that, not to my memory."

"And he didn't say he lay down again?"

"No, sir."

Burritt says, "Mr. Heikkila, I am finding more holes in your memory and your notes than I see in a slice of Swiss cheese!"

The judge says sternly, "Mr. Burritt, that statement is unprofessional and uncalled for. One more outburst like that and I'll find you in contempt! Do you understand?"

"Yes, Your Honor. I apologize. May I continue?"

The judge says, "Yes — if you are able to maintain some degree of professional decorum."

Burritt humbly says, "Thank you, Your Honor."

Alex thinks, *I can't say I disagree with you, William. But what will the jury think about your little outburst? You should try to maintain friendly relationships with the members of the jury. That's what's most important here!*

Burritt continues by asking Heikkila, "Where did he say he was when he laid down?"

"In the field."

"Where in the field?"

"He didn't state."

"Did you ask him?"

"No, sir."

"Did you ask him what time it was when he woke up?"

"Yes."

"What?"

"I asked him when he woke up the next morning."

"He said he woke up the next morning. Is that what he said?"

"That's what he said."

"And he was in the field."

"Yes."

"So, he told you that he lay down, went to sleep, woke up the next morning, and found himself out in the field. That's right?"

"Yes, sir."

"And then he went home, did he?"

"I remember he went in the saloon and drank some more on Saturday."

"He said he went into a saloon again, got some more booze, had some more to drink, and lay in the field again."

"Yes."

"Now, didn't he tell you when he woke up in the morning, the first night he laid out and found himself in the field, that he got up, went to a saloon and got some more to drink, didn't he?"

"Yes."

"And he told you he went to a saloon in Little Lake, didn't he?"

"No, sir."

"Didn't he tell you he walked from wherever he was laying in the field, to Little Lake, got there before the saloon opened, went in the saloon at Little Lake, and got some more to drink?"

"No, sir."

"He didn't tell you where the saloon was?" Burritt asks.

"He told me as soon as he woke up, he went to the saloon."

"He didn't say where the saloon was?"

"No."

"He merely said when he woke up, he got up and went to the saloon and got some more drink. Is that right?"

"Yes, sir."

"And he said he got drunk again, didn't he?"

"Yes."

"And he said that he went out into the bush again."

"Yes, sir."

"And he said he lay around in the bush or in the field or somewhere until it was time to go home, didn't he?"

"Yes, sir."

"And he then took a train and went to Rumley, didn't he?"

"He didn't tell me whether he took the train or not. In fact, I didn't know where Rumley was."

"He said he lay in the field until it was time to go home, he took the train, and went to his brother Bill's?"

"No sir, he didn't say anything about a train."

Burritt is irritated at Heikkila's poor responses to his questions and throws his hands in the air in a dismissive gesture as he walks back to the defense table.

Alex thinks, *That was some grilling you gave him, Burritt. Where will it lead?*

Burritt shifts gears and asks Heikkila about the Lahnala home. "Now, you went out to the August Lahnala home on the morning of the sixth of September, did you?"

"Yes, sir."

"That was the morning after the murder was supposed to have been committed."

"Yes, sir."

"You made an examination around the house, didn't you, the premises?"

"Yes, sir."

"And did you find any footprints outside the house?"

"Yes."

"Where?"

"There were all kinds of footprints around there."

"Did you measure them?"

"No, sir."

"Did you find any places where anyone had been laying down or standing up or any evidence of that kind around the house?"

"Just a short distance from the house, it seemed as though somebody lay in the field there. That's the oat field."

"You found some spot out near the oat field where it looked as if somebody had been laying down."

"Yes, sir."

"But it was only a matter of conjecture as to whether anybody had been there or not?"

"Yes, sir."

"It could have been a deer that made it look like that?"

"Yes, sir."

"Did you look for deer hoof marks?"

"Yes, but we did not see any."

Burritt says, "So, maybe it wasn't a deer after all."

Continuing, Burritt asks, "Did you make an examination around the telephone pole that the wire was cut from?"

Heikkila replies, "Yes, sir."

"And around the brace post?"

"Yes, sir."

"And you say you measured the foot track you found there?"

"Yes, sir."

"And the wire represents the length of that foot track as it was impressed in the plowed ground?"

"Yes sir. The left foot."

"When you were measuring that track, why didn't you get a rule or something to measure it accurately so you would know its length?"

"We were very busy at the time. We were anxious to get on the trail of the party that committed this deed and did it hastily."

"You was in a hurry?"

"Not very excited."

"Why didn't you get a rule or tape to measure the length of the foot track so you would know how long it was by accurate measurement from point to point? Because you was in a hurry?"

"To a certain extent, yes."

"Now, did you see any other tracks?"

"No, sir."

"Do you know a Jacob Miller who might be associated with this case?"

"Yes, sir."

"You was on his trail."

"Yes, sir."

"What did you hear about Miller?"

"Well, we heard that he threatened August Lahnala."

"Did you investigate that angle?"

"I followed up and visited with Miller. He told me August owed him some money because he borrowed a horse from Miller. The horse died, but Miller didn't seem too upset about it. Then he just about passed out in front of me. He said he hasn't been feeling good and told me he has to get to the bathroom. Then he closed the door in my face. I figured I'd get back to him after he felt better, and I came back to the office."

"Did you ever do more follow-up with Miller?"

"No. John Lahnala was arrested, and I started to work on that part of the case."

"You ever hear of a fellow by the name of Jack Lacy?"

"Yes, sir."

"Who was he?"

"I understand that he served time in Ionia State Prison."

"Did you look him up, try to get any further information on him?"

"Yes sir, we took the matter up. We thought it was important at that time, but we were convinced later it was not, so we stopped that part of the investigation."

"What changed your mind of the importance of this part of the investigation?"

"Well, the defendant was arrested, so we focused more on that part of the investigation."

"You stopped the part of the investigation about Lacy?"

"Yes."

"Now, you understood that this man Lacy was from Ontonagon County and went to the penitentiary?"

"Yes, sir."

"And Lahnala, the deceased, had been a witness in the case against him?"

"I understand he was."

"You understood that Lacy spent a long time in the penitentiary and might be looking for revenge?"

"Yes, sir. We figured somebody must have had a grudge against Lahnala."

"And that was the theory of your investigation against both Miller and Lacy?"

"Yes, sir."

"And you didn't do any more follow-up on either Miller or Lacy. When John Lahnala was arrested, you just focused the investigation on him?"

"Yes, sir."

REDIRECT EXAMINATION BY GALBRAITH

Galbraith asks, "Was the measurement that you made of the footprint by means of this wire an exact measurement?"

Heikkila responds, "Yes, sir. The toe part was a little blurred, as though it had been worn."

Turning his attention to Lacy, Galbraith asks, "From whom did you get the information regarding this man Lacy?"

"From Mrs. Lahnala and Charles Lahnala."

"Who is Charles Lahnala?"

"A brother to the man that's dead."

"You investigated these parties until such time as you satisfied yourself that they were —"

Burritt objects, "The question is incompetent."

Galbraith replies, "They would be incompetent except as they have been made so by the course of cross-examination."

The Court says, "Yes. I think I will overrule the objection."

Burritt says, "Note an exception."

The Court reads the last question, and Burritt says, "Further objection, question is leading."

The judge replies, "I will sustain that objection."

Galbraith continues, "Calling your attention to this man, Lacy. Why did you not continue further investigation of that case?"

Burritt objects, "I object to that as immaterial, incompetent."

The Court says, "I think they have the right to explain."

Burritt says, "Note an exception."

Alex says to himself, *Another exception?!* As Alex looks at the jury, he thinks he sees a certain hardness setting in on some faces as they look at Burritt. Then they look back at Heikkila.

Heikkila answers the question. "We were to get into communication with the Ontonagon sheriff's office about this Lacy, but after we arrested John Lahnala, we started to work on that part of the case."

Galbraith asks, "Why didn't you pursue the investigation of the case of this man, Miller, further?"

"Because he was very sick at the time we went there that morning, and he gave a good account of himself."

Burritt objects, saying the testimony is incompetent, but the Court overrules.

Burritt gets frustrated because the Court seems to disregard his objections. If the verdict in this case is not favorable to his client, he senses he will have a good opportunity to appeal to a higher court. To show he doesn't agree with this ruling, he again says, "Exception."

Heikkila answers, "I wasn't detailed on that part to look this man up. I think one of the other officers was detailed on that part. There was so many different rumors running around, the sheriff put different officers on different rumors."

"The other investigations were made by other officers, of which you have no personal knowledge."

"Yes, sir."

William hears Barney cough, which is a hint to his father to have a short sidebar discussion. Barney whispers in his father's ear, "Don't forget to ask him about who owned the pliers."

RECROSS-EXAMINATION BY BURRITT

Burritt asks Heikkila, "Now, did you try to determine who owned the pliers you found the morning after the murder at the base of the pole?"

"We did not."

"Did you suspect that the pliers you found at the base of the pole might have been used by the murderer to cut the wire at the top of the pole?"

"Yes, we thought so. But we also wanted to secure the evidence in the kitchen where the body was."

"Did you *ever* try to determine who owned the pliers?"

"We thought they must have been owned by John Lahnala."

"You developed that theory after you heard that John was arrested. Is that true?"

"Yes."

"Until he was arrested, you had no idea who owned them. Is that true?"

"Yes."

Burritt says, "We have no more questions."

At this point, Alex's attention is interrupted as Hilda whispers to him, "This is interesting to me, and I really don't want to leave. But Ruth, the babysitter, told me yesterday that she has other business to tend to, so I should get home."

Alex understands and says, "See you later."

Alex makes a mental note. "I must remember to talk to Burritt about the Sheriff's office not following up on Lacy and the numerous times that Heikkila said he didn't remember what John told him. What kind of investigator is he?"

Chapter 13
William Lucas Testimony

Mr. Galbraith next called for Deputy Sheriff William G. Lucas to take the stand.

Mr. Lucas walked to the stand and displayed a more confident manner than Undersheriff Heikkila. After he identified himself, he testified that he made a trip to Rumley three days after August Lahnala was murdered, to talk to Bill and John Lahnala; that he overheard a discussion about a murder while he was in the Marquette train depot; that he learned that the men talking were Bill and John Lahnala; and that the family was traveling to Houghton to attend August's funeral.

He testified that he got into a discussion with John and asked if John was in Rumley continuously since the previous Thursday, September 3, and John said he was not. When asked, John explained that he and Bill went to look for work on Thursday; that he, John, was hired by Charles Lindeman, the railroad section man at Little Lake and spent the night at Lindeman's house; that on Friday, he and Lindeman went to New Swanzy and got drunk; that he wasn't feeling well, so he went into a field to sleep; that he woke in the dark, so he slept until morning; and that on Saturday, he went to his brother Bill's house.

Lucas then arrested John for further investigation, took him to the Houghton County Jail, and at the jail, John gave a statement which was like what he said on the train.

Galbraith asked, "Did you make any further investigation of the matter?"

Lucas replied, "I did. Bill Lahnala and his family went home after the funeral on September 9. I left for the Rumley area the next day, September 10."

"Did you go to Bill Lahnala's house?"

"I did."

“When you were earlier talking to John, did he make any statements about the ownership of a pistol?”

“He said he had a gun in Bill’s house, and he hadn’t used it since July fourth.”

“Did you look for and find the gun?”

“I did.”

“Where did you find the gun?”

“It was at Bill’s house, in his tool chest.”

Galbraith picks up a pistol and asks for it to be marked People’s Exhibit 11. It is a Colt .32-caliber automatic.

He asks Lucas, “I ask if this is the gun you found?”

“Yes, sir. It looks like the gun.”

“When you found the gun, was it loaded?”

“Yes, sir, it was.”

“Is the clip or magazine part of the gun?”

“Yes. It was in the gun when I found it.”

Galbraith says he’d feel better if the clip was separated from the gun. The clip is removed from the gun as he asks for the gun and clip to be marked People’s Exhibits 11 and 12.

Burritt says, “We object to it for the following reason. There is no testimony in the case tending in any way to connect it with the issue involved in this case.”

Alex thinks, *Good point!*

The Court overrules the objection. Burritt takes another exception.

Alex looks at the jury, and three men adjust themselves in their seats.

CROSS-EXAMINATION BY BURRITT

"Now, you said you got the gun from Bill Lahnala's house."

"Yes."

"That's all you know about it."

"Yes."

Burritt renews his objection, saying, "We object to it for the reason that there is no evidence the gun is connected in this case."

The Court replies, "I will admit the gun and magazine in evidence."

Burritt says, "Note an exception."

Burritt asks Lucas questions to recap his testimony. There being no notable differences from what he just testified, Burritt says, "Thank you. I think we are through."

Galbraith says, "I'd like to call Herbert Lahnala."

Judge O'Brien interjects, "It is getting rather late, and we got a lot accomplished today. Let's adjourn until tomorrow."

After court is adjourned, Alex asks the Burritt team if he could briefly meet with them, and they say, "Of course!"

After the courtroom is empty, Alex says, "Heikkila doesn't seem to remember much of what John told him. He isn't very thorough for somebody who is investigating a murder. He didn't even try to determine who owned the pliers at the base of the pole! I'm glad you asked about that."

William agrees. "Unfortunately, I've seen similar things before. And Barney reminded me to ask about the pliers when we had our little sidebar discussion."

Alex asks, "Do you think getting into all the details will cause the jury to believe that the prosecution really has its ducks lined up, so to speak? Won't that hurt our case?"

William replies, "I don't know what the jury knows about the overall story. They need to know it. If I objected, they'd have to find out some other way. I didn't want those twelve men to think I was betraying a lack of candor and trying to hide the truth."

"Ahhh, that makes sense," Alex responds.

"I'm also wondering if it's common for the judge to overrule as many objections as you've had?" Alex asks.

William replies, "The Court seems to be leaning a little toward the prosecution's side of things. All I can do is make our position known. Maybe things will change as the trial proceeds."

Alex thanks the Burritt team for the meeting and says he's heading home. As he walks outside, he doesn't know what to think of the day's proceedings. In his mind, Lucas seemed to jump the gun by arresting John on only his gut feeling. Alex thinks Heikkila hardly qualifies to be a murder investigator, based on his responses to William's questions. Also, the judge seems to have a definite lean toward the prosecution. He wonders if this is what 'Copper Country justice' really looks like. The only professionals Alex saw today were the defense lawyers.

But he doesn't like the attitude that William Burritt seems to have. Why does he have so many objections and exceptions? Alex has watched the jurors, and they don't seem to like it either. And the way Burritt badgered Heikkila. He gets the feeling that the jurors might be developing a negative impression of Burritt. If that's the case, Alex wonders if Burritt's antics might be biasing the jury against John also.

When he arrives home that afternoon, Hilda asks, "What did I miss this afternoon?"

Alex says, "Deputy Lucas testified that he was heading to the Rumley area to talk to John and Bill on September 8, but at the Marquette train depot, he overheard them talking about a shooting. Lucas then went into his meeting with John and the others at the depot. He suspects John was somehow involved in the murder of your father. He asked John if he was in Rumley continuously since Thursday, and John said "No", which was true. He was away from Rumley looking for work. After hearing John's reply, Lucas arrested him on the train. I couldn't believe it!

"I'm also getting concerned about the way William Burritt is conducting the case for the defense. He seems to be objecting more than I ever expected a lawyer to object and taking more exceptions also. I've watched a couple of men in the jury, and they have appeared frustrated also. The jurors don't know the law as well as the judge and lawyers do. The trial is getting pretty technical, and I'm afraid it is getting away from the simple facts of the case. I'm not sure I like Burritt's approach!"

Hilda replied, "That's an interesting observation. I'll be with you at the courthouse tomorrow, at least for the morning, and see if I get the same impression. But right now, I'm tired and am going to bed. Good night."

Chapter 14
Herbie, Greta, LaBine, Johnson Testimony

Alex wakes early so he can get a jump on his daily chores. Hilda also gets up early so she can make breakfast, feed Ernie, and get her girls ready for the day. The girls grumble when they realize that their mom will be gone for most of the day. But their babysitter will be a well-loved neighbor, so that thought soothes them.

As Alex and Hilda drive to Houghton, there is a realization that most people will never experience what they're going through. They can't think of anyone who had a relative accused of murder. Let alone the murder of their father.

They talk about John's upbeat attitude so far during the trial. "He has always accepted whatever comes his way." says Hilda.

"He certainly has a strong mental attitude and much faith in his legal team. Stronger than mine, I think." says Alex.

"I think he's learned about a positive attitude from you, Alex." says his wife. "That's one of the reasons I fell in love with you!"

Alex blushes and puts his hand on Hilda's hand as they drive quietly toward the courthouse.

They enter the courthouse and take their seats in the courtroom. The bailiff calls the court to order, and Mr. Galbraith calls his first witness of the day — Hilda's young brother.

TESTIMONY OF HERBERT LAHNALA

Herbert Lahnala is produced and sworn on behalf of the People and is examined in chief by Mr. Galbraith.

The Court asks, "What grade are you in, Herbert?"

Herbert replies, "I don't know what grade. I went to school, but I never go to school this winter or last winter."

The Court asks, "Do you understand what it means to take an oath?"

Herbert replies, "I want to talk Finn."

The Court recognizes that Herbert's English skills are not strong and agrees to allow him to testify in Finnish.

In response to Galbraith's questions, Herbert says he was at home when his father was killed. Earlier that day, they were making hay. Herbert is asked what he did after haying and he replies, "We had to get the cows."

Galbraith asks, "When you say, 'we had to get the cows', who do you mean?"

"Me and Arthur."

Galbraith asks, "Who is he?"

"My younger brother."

Galbraith continues, "What is his age?"

"I don't know. Ask my mother."

There is a slight giggle in the courtroom. Galbraith says, "I just might!"

He then continues, "Did you and Arthur milk the cows that night?"

"We milked the cows with my mother."

Herbert testifies that in the evening, everybody went upstairs to bed except his father, who went to Hermanson's store to get a few items. When his father came home at eight thirty, Herbert was upstairs repairing a shoe. He heard his father walking downstairs and heard some noise in the kitchen shed. Herbert heard the kitchen door open, three shots, his father yelled, and something heavy fell to the floor. His mother and the others went downstairs and found his father on the kitchen floor, apparently dead. The family tried to call for help, but the telephone didn't work. Everybody was afraid to go outside because they might get shot, so they covered his father's body with a sheet, and after a while, they all went back upstairs. But nobody slept.

A little after five o'clock the next morning, Herbert's mother told him to run the two miles to Alex Olson's home because Alex is married to Herbert's older sister, Hilda, and Alex will know what to do. After Herbert got to Olson's house, he and Alex came back to the Lahnala home.

Galbraith asks where the other Lahnala children were, and Herbert tells him. Galbraith asks specifically where John is living, and Herbert said he's living in Rumley.

When asked how John and his father got along, Herbert said their father was "cranky" with all the kids, but otherwise, John and his father got along fine. Herbert verified that his father wouldn't buy any nice clothes for John, and John had talked to his father many times about that. John left home and got a job because he didn't get any clothes or spending money from his father. But he did come home to help his father do the haying that summer.

Mr. Galbraith asks Herbert about the pliers, which are People's Exhibit 8, and Herbert said he saw them when Mr. Heikkila found them the day his father was killed. But he never saw them before that day.

Herbert's testimony lasted all morning, partially due to the length of time it took for the translation of questions from English to Finnish and translating Herbert's Finnish answers to English.

The Court says, "We've been sitting for a long time, so let's adjourn for lunch. Court is adjourned until 12:30 p.m. today."

Hilda says, "I'd like to stay and hear what Mother has to say, but I can't stay any longer. I've heard Herbie testify. Now I must get home to take care of things there."

Alex gives her a hug and says, "Okay, I'll take good notes! I'll see you at home this afternoon."

Alex sits at the defense counsel table because the Burritts don't take a break for lunch. The Burritts stay at their table while the courtroom empties, but many spectators stay in the courtroom. Alex is surprised. He supposes that this legal spectacle is something new to them, and they don't want to lose their vantage points. The Burritt team then proceeds to the defense meeting room, just off the courtroom, to discuss how the trial is going.

TESTIMONY OF MRS. GRETA LAHNALA

When the court reconvenes after lunch, Mr. Galbraith calls for Mrs. Greta Lahnala, the wife of the murder victim. Her lengthy testimony is almost identical to her son Herbie's testimony and reinforces what he said.

TESTIMONY OF DR. ALFRED LABINE

Dr. Alfred LaBine, the Houghton County Physician when Lahnala was killed, testifies that he performed the autopsy on August Lahnala. He found a single gunshot wound just beneath the collar bone. He traced the bullet through the right lung, where it struck the anterior part of the spine and came to rest under the ribs on the right side. He confirms that the bullet is the cause of death.

Alex thinks, *That testimony was quick! I'm glad Burritt didn't have any objections, but Dr. LaBine's findings were pretty straightforward.*

TESTIMONY OF FRED JOHNSON

Mr. Galbraith for the People says, "I call Fred Johnson."

After taking the stand, Mr. Johnson testifies that he was at Gekas' Candy Kitchen the evening of September 4, 1914, entertaining Selma Hermanson, Elizabeth Olson, and Hilja Olson. He says he was eating ice cream with the girls when Selma said, "There is John Lahnala." Johnson says he turned his head and saw him standing there just before he walked out.

Under cross-examination, Burritt gets Johnson to admit he never spent much time with John Lahnala, and only thought it was Lahnala when his attention was called to it. Johnson admits that he hadn't seen Lahnala for about a year and infrequently before that. Burritt also gets him to admit that his attention was on the girls he was entertaining. He didn't have any idea of how many people entered and left the Candy Kitchen while he was there.

Burritt asks Johnson, "Now, when you had the girls with you, you were so engaged with the girls, you thought you was pretty well fixed, didn't you? They attracted your entire attention, didn't they?"

Johnson replies, "I know what I am doing, even when I am with women," which drew some laughter from the courtroom.

After court is adjourned for the day, Alex meets with the legal team. He listens intently while William and Barney talk about keeping an eye on individual jury members to see if any of them have facial expressions that might suggest which way they are leaning — toward the prosecution or toward the defense.

Alex asks, "Will someone explain this to me, please?"

William explains, "Sometimes jury members will favor one side or the other, defense or prosecution, and the way they are leaning can be used by the defense team to bolster their case. If a 'favorite' juror is recognized, perhaps the defense can 'play' to that juror and influence the outcome of the case."

Alex wonders if this concept is ethical and convinces himself that it is.

Barney says, "The third juror from the left in the back row seems to be the most interested in what is happening in the courtroom. He is the most attentive and nods his head occasionally when you make a good point, Dad. He would be a good gauge on how our case is being accepted."

Alex says, "You guys are busy following the more technical legal points in the case, so I'll also keep my eyes on the jury and, specifically, number three."

Alex looks for an opportunity to talk to Barney alone.

William is momentarily called aside by a reporter who wants to get his impressions of how the trial is proceeding thus far. Alex takes the opening to talk to Barney.

"I'm concerned about the impact your father's many exceptions might have on the jury. It looked like most of the jury members didn't react favorably when William requested an exception as Galbraith was questioning Heikkila."

Barney says, "This is a balancing act of sorts. A good defense lawyer will not want to do anything which might cause the jury to lean toward the prosecution. But on the other hand, that lawyer will also want to preserve as many chances as possible for a new trial through the appeals process in case the verdict is for the prosecution."

Alex responds, "I just hope that the use of exceptions doesn't actually drive a juror, or jurors, to the prosecution side." Alex then excuses himself, saying he must get home.

As Alex drives home that afternoon, he realizes that Hilda will want to know how her mother did on the witness stand. As soon as he gets in the door, he removes his coat, sits down with Hilda, and says, "Your mother did well. Her testimony was a repetition of what Herbie said. She agreed with Herbie and said your father got along well with John, but August would not buy John any new clothes. She didn't add much except to give her own thoughts on what happened. As your father's wife, she had a slightly different perspective, of course, and that was obvious. She did add that she opened your father's shirt and saw some blood on his chest.

"It was also interesting because Fred Johnson testified about what he *thinks* he saw at Gekas' Candy Kitchen. William Burritt got Fred to admit that he hadn't seen John in a long time. He also asked him about how positive he is that it was John he saw. Fred said, 'I thought it was him.' William got him to admit he was preoccupied with the women he was entertaining. But Fred said he wasn't 'too preoccupied' and said, 'I know what I am doing when I'm with women.' That caused a little laughter in the courtroom." Hilda chuckled.

Alex also introduces Hilda to the concept of a favorite juror, which William and Barney talked about in their afternoon meeting. "Barney suggested a specific juror to watch, so I agreed to keep an eye on him." Hilda is surprised that lawyers could use such a tactic.

Alex says, "All's fair in love and war! This isn't exactly a war, but there are definitely two sides, and at least one life is at risk. So, the analogy fits — although it might be a loose fit."

Hilda has several questions, but after about half an hour, the discussion goes elsewhere and she is satisfied with Alex's report.

Chapter 15
Elizabeth, Hilja, Lindeman Testimony

TESTIMONY OF ELIZABETH OLSON

At court the next morning, Alex sits up in his seat when his sister Elizabeth is called to the stand. He thinks, *This should be interesting — to me at least!*

After taking her seat on the witness stand, Galbraith asks her name to confirm she is Alex's sister. She testifies she was at the Candy Kitchen with Selma Hermanson, her sister Hilja, and Fred Johnson. She also says she saw John Lahnala at the Candy Kitchen that evening.

Well, well! Alex thinks. *I believe that John was in the Rumley area and you're testifying that you saw him in Houghton. Obviously, one of us doesn't know the truth. I know it has to be you, sister!*

She says her attention was directed to the man when Selma said, "There is John Lahnala." Elizabeth says she glimpsed the man from the side but didn't watch him, so she didn't know what he was doing.

Under cross-examination, Burritt gets her to admit her attention was with the people at her table and the ice cream she was eating. Burritt asks if she knows Evert Walitalo, and she confirms that she does.

Burritt asks, "Did you ever tell Evert Walitalo that you wasn't certain it was John. You just thought it was John when you saw him there but couldn't swear to it? Did you tell him that or words to that effect?"

She replies, "No, I never told him that."

Burritt says he has no more questions at this time.

Alex is thinking "William knows something that I don't know." He doesn't understand what William is doing. Does William know something about a discussion Elizabeth had with Walitalo? Or is he simply grasping at straws? If William thinks that Elizabeth is not telling the truth, why doesn't he pursue that line of questioning? Alex hopes William can put some meat on the bones of what appears to be his speculation.

TESTIMONY OF HILJA OLSON

Mr. Galbraith next calls Hilja Olson to the stand. Hilja walks to the stand with her chin raised, in an obvious attempt at belligerence. Alex is trying to control his nerves, but that's not easy when his most opinionated sister is called for the prosecution. He thinks, *Where will this end? What kind of family rift will this cause? Oh, Lord!*

In reply to Galbraith's questioning, she confirms that she is seventeen years old and was at the Candy Kitchen on September 4, 1914, with Selma Hermanson, her sister Elizabeth Olson, and Fred Johnson. She also says she saw John Lahnala at the Candy Kitchen that evening.

Like her sister, Hilja says Selma Hermanson drew her attention to the man. Also, like Elizabeth, she said she only had a side view of him. Hilja admits she never went to school with John, had not seen him for more than a year prior to last September, and had only seen him once or twice in two or three years.

Under cross-examination, Hilja adjusts herself in the stand and looks like she's ready to give Burritt 'what for'. Burritt asks, "Now, since the night you think you saw John at the Candy Kitchen, after you went away from there, you talked it over with the girls, didn't you?"

"No, sir."

Burritt obviously knows more about this than Alex does. Burritt's brows drop over his eyes a bit as he challenges, "Never did, eh? Now, after talking the matter over with the girls and after talking with the sheriff or some of the officers, then your belief that the person you saw there was John was strengthened, wasn't it?"

"I don't know. I saw him there, and I thought it was him."

"Then your testimony here today is based on what you saw that night, your talk with the girls, your talk with the officers, and your talk with Johnson. Your testimony is based on all those things, which has strengthened you so that you now think you saw him?"

"Yes, sir."

Alex thinks, *This is a positive development! I wonder if Burritt can expand on it?*

Burritt asks, "Do you know Evert Walitalo?"

"Yes, I know him."

"Did you ever tell Evert Walitalo that you wasn't certain it was John, you just thought it was John when you saw him there, and couldn't swear to it? Did you tell him that or words to that effect?"

"No, I never told him that."

With dropped brows, Burritt asks, "Never did, eh?"

Burritt continues, "Do you know Mrs. Wayrynen?"

"Yes, sir."

"Where does she live?"

"She lives at the Canal."

"You have talked to her about this matter, haven't you?"

"I can't remember, maybe I have."

"Didn't you tell Mrs. Wayrynen that you weren't sure that it was John?"

"I can't remember what I told her."

"Did you tell her, 'I thought it was him I saw. But he looked like a stranger. If he had said good day or had spoken, then I might have been sure.' Didn't you say that, or words to that effect, to Mrs. Wayrynen?"

"Yes sir, but just the same I will keep it in my mind all the time that it was him."

"But you told her you wasn't sure; if he had spoken, you would have been more sure?"

"Of course, I can't swear it was him."

"You can't say for certain, can you?"

"I couldn't say for certain."

"Didn't you say to Mrs. Wayrynen, 'I am not sure it was John.' You told her you wasn't sure it was John, didn't you?"

"Yes, sir."

Well! Alex thinks. *This could be the 'meat' I was looking for. This shoots a large hole in Hilja's testimony. I wonder how much this will impact the outcome of the trial. I also wonder how much this will impact Hilja's relationship with my wife and the rest of the Lahnala family. And what does the jury think? Juror number three has a surprised look on his face, which I read as a good sign. It looks like number three is in disbelief that Hilja was called to be a witness for the prosecution. Shooting holes in Hilja's testimony was so easy, it makes it appear like even the prosecution doesn't believe that John killed August. I wish William would have taken this tack with Elizabeth also! I wonder why he didn't.*

TESTIMONY OF CHARLES LINDEMAN

After being sworn, Lindeman says he lives in Old Swanzy and is the section foreman on the railroad near Little Lake.

He says he saw John Lahnala in the late afternoon at the train depot in Little Lake on September 3, 1914. He asked John if he wanted to work on the section, and he said he did. Lindeman hired him, they went to Old Swanzy, and Lahnala had dinner with him at the section house. John spent the night at the section house. The next morning, after breakfast, Lindeman, John, and fellas called Swanson, Soderstrom, and Fredrickson went to Princeton and had a drink. Lindeman said they were all sober because they can't get drunk when they're working. Then they went to LaRochelle's saloon in New Swanzy and had more to drink before heading back to the section house for noon lunch. Lindeman didn't see Lahnala after lunch.

Burritt doesn't have any questions, so the Court adjourns for the day.

As Alex is driving home for the evening, he wonders if they made the right decision in hiring the Burritt team.

Would another attorney be taking the same course and asking the same questions? But he also realizes that William Burritt hasn't had an opportunity to present the case for the defense. William also has some tricks up his sleeve — like getting Hilja and Elizabeth to back away from their identification of John at the candy store. Alex figures he must reserve judgment until things play out more.

Alex is looking forward to getting home to talk with his wife. As he nears the house, he sees Hilda in the doorway window. She is undoubtedly wondering how the trial went today.

As he enters the kitchen, before Hilda can ask any questions, Alex notices the smell of Finnish cardamom sweetbread, known locally as *nisu*. "You've been baking today!" he says. "That smells delicious!"

"And it's still warm from the oven!" replies Hilda.

"I'll have two pieces with a coffee, please." Alex requests, hoping that Hilda will serve him. He is somewhat surprised when she does.

He asks her, "Were there any problems with the children doing my chores today?"

Hilda replied, "Not really. The children are a little slower than you when you're doing the work, but that's to be expected because they don't have your routine. More important, how did the trial go today?"

"My sisters, Elizabeth and Hilia, were on the stand today. Boy, was I nervous. I was pleased with William's performance when he cross-examined them. After court was adjourned, I met with him and told him, 'You did a good job today shooting holes in the testimony of my sisters.' Burritt replied, 'Yes, that went well. I hope the jury was listening. I only wish that they weren't your sisters because I can see where that might cause some difficulty in your relationship with them. It would also be great if the others that were at Gekas' could be less sure of their identification of John. But we will have opportunities.'"

Alex continues, "I'm afraid William Burritt made them look foolish. Let me tell you what happened. When the girls and Fred Johnson were at the candy store, Selma Hermanson said, 'Look, John Lahnala.' Both Elizabeth and Hilja said they *thought* it looked like him. But Hilja said she only saw him for a moment and only had a side view. William then got her to admit that her subsequent discussions with the other girls and with the sheriff's office strengthened her belief that it was John. After a few more questions, she admitted that she couldn't swear it was John who she saw.

"Elizabeth said almost the same thing. She *thought* it was John she saw. But Burritt didn't do as much follow-up with her as he did with Hilja. I met with him briefly after court adjourned for the day, and he said more will come out on this when he starts his defense."

"That's interesting!" says Hilda. "It sounds like it was a good day for John's defense."

Alex bares his soul. "I'm troubled with this whole thing."

"I'm sure John is innocent and that he was in Rumley when your pa was killed. Yet my own sisters are testifying that they saw him in town. I really don't know what to think. Then Burritt gets them to admit that they didn't see what they've told other people they've seen. I'm fighting a battle against my own family!"

Hilda agrees. "I understand your feelings. I'm sure this will strain our relationships. And I wonder if your sisters will be branded as liars because of their testimony."

After a contemplative moment or two, Alex continues with his daily report. "Dr. LaBine also was questioned and talked about how he traced the killing bullet in your father's body."

Hilda remarks, "I don't need to know about that!"

Alex replies, "I agree, but LaBine confirmed it was the cause of his death."

Alex continues, "Galbraith called Charles Lindeman, who testified about his hiring of John at the railroad depot in Little Lake. He talked about the crew going to a saloon, having some drinks, John spending the night at the section house, and so on. His testimony reinforces what we've heard from John and others. Overall, it was a pretty good day, I think."

Alex then says he must check that everything is alright with the cattle in the barn and do a few chores. After eating a late dinner, Alex has another cup of coffee with nisu. "I'm beat," Alex says. "I need to get some sleep."

Hilda gives Alex a kiss on the cheek. "Thanks for a good report on today's events at court." Trying to relieve his anxiety, she adds, "Remember that you're not responsible for what your sisters or others say in court. We know the truth. Good night."

Chapter 16
Zurcher, Vertriga, Solmonson Testimony

On Friday, February 19, Alex and Hilda are awake earlier than normal so he can get some chores done before driving to Houghton for resumption of the trial. It is a freezing morning, but 'Super Lake' kept the temperature a bit more reasonable near her shores. Alex is thankful that there was very little fresh snowfall overnight.

As he drives to the courthouse, Alex wonders what surprises will surface today.

When court convenes for the day, Mr. Galbraith calls for John Zurcher.

TESTIMONY OF JOHN ZURCHER

John Zurcher testifies that he's in the dairy business on Canal Road. He also verifies that he knows Bill and John Lahnala and also knew their father. He confirms that Bill worked for him continuously for about two years and lived on the Zurcher farm during most of that time. He also says John worked for him for a while. Zurcher testifies that John called his father a son of a bitch when August was in jail for drunkenness, but he never heard John make any threats toward August.

Burritt asks if Zurcher ever had any problems with the Lahnala boys. Zurcher says he did not.

TESTIMONY OF MRS. VERTRIGA LAHNALA THROUGH AN INTERPRETER

Mrs. Vertriga Lahnala, examined by Mr. Galbraith, testifies that her husband, Enoch, is a brother of the late August Lahnala. She said she and Enoch visited August and Greta, and the men went out of the house to look at the farm.

While they were gone, Greta said, "August will keep the hired men to do the work and pay them, but he cannot keep his own children at home and get along with them like other people."

John heard this and said, "Why must Father be that way?"

But Vertriga says she never heard any cross words between John and August.

TESTIMONY OF HILDA SOLMONSON

Mr. Galbraith calls Miss Hilda Solmonson, who testifies she has known John Lahnala since they were children. She says she also worked with John at Zurcher's dairy farm. Sometimes when she was with John, he would talk about his father, calling him "red whiskers" and "slouch." Selma said she visited John once when John was staying in the house rented by Bill at Zurcher's. John went into Bill's bedroom, produced a .32-caliber pistol, and said, "With this I will bore that slouch through."

She confirms that John found fault with his father because August sometimes beat his mother. Through it all, however, John and August were peaceful with each other. She said Bill purchased the pistol because he carried money for Zurcher, and he wanted protection.

Chapter 17
Ollie, Kuru, Alina, Hilda O. Testimony

TESTIMONY OF WILLIAM OLLIE

After being called to testify, William Ollie walks to the witness stand and takes the seat. He confirms that he is married to Alina Lahnala, John's sister, and says he has lived near Rumley since April 1914. John Lahnala and his brother, Bill, went with him when he moved to Rumley.

William confirms that on Sunday, September 6, the brothers came to his house around 8:00 a.m. to see if he wanted to go hunting. He couldn't go because he had to work getting the walls of his house insulated for the coming winter. William said there were big cracks along the walls. He recalled John coming into the house for a drink when they returned around noon. After noon, William says the brothers brought him a sack full of moss for chinking the walls. William confirms that John said in a discussion they had that he would not let his father in his house if he came to visit.

On Monday evening, September 7, William said Bill received a telegram saying August was killed. Bill and John came to Ollie's home to share the news. It was completely dark in William's house because he didn't have any oil for lights, so he couldn't see any of August's children crying. But he heard his wife crying.

William testified that he didn't attend August's funeral.

But his wife, Alina, their children, Bill and his wife, Hannah, and their children, and John traveled together to the funeral. They left home on Tuesday, September 8.

TESTIMONY OF MRS. EVA KURU THROUGH AN INTERPRETER

Mr. Galbraith asks, "Do you know Mrs. August Lahnala?"

Mrs. Kuru replies, "Yes."

"Was Mrs. Lahnala to your place on the eighteenth of October last?"

"Yes."

"What did you and Mrs. Lahnala talk about at that time?"

"I wanted to tell her what August told me about his enemies."

Burritt objected, saying, "Any talk between this witness and the deceased about his enemies is hearsay and incompetent."

Alex is thinking, *What are you objecting to, Burritt? Why not let the jury know about his enemies? Wouldn't that benefit John?*

Galbraith says, "We are not following it any further."

The Court says, "Strike out the testimony regarding August's enemies."

Galbraith says, "Your witness, Mr. Burritt."

Burritt says, "I have no questions of Mrs. Kuru."

After the court adjourns for the day, Alex has a meeting with William and Barney. Alex asks William, "Why did you object to Mrs. Kuru talking about August's enemies? Wouldn't our case benefit if the jury learned about his enemies?"

To Alex's surprise, William agrees, saying, "Perhaps I was a little hasty with my objection. But I didn't want Mrs. Kuru to say John's name and have the jury associate John's name with the word 'enemies'. That would not be good. I'd like to control the paintbrush, so to speak, so we can control the picture which is presented to the jury."

Alex says, "You guys really know how to handle different situations in the courtroom. I would never have thought of that. In any event, it seems Galbraith was eager to strike that testimony. Can Mrs. Kuru's testimony regarding August's enemies be explored later in the trial?"

"Perhaps I can get into that when the defense case starts." says William.

For the umpteenth time, Alex has doubts about the legal team he and Hilda have hired to defend John. He is thinking, *I don't agree with William's analysis of things. It seems to me that talk of August's enemies would surely benefit John. Many witnesses have already said that John and his father got along fine so testimony already shows that they were not enemies.*

And all these exceptions are clearly rubbing the judge the wrong way. They may also be making the jurors think the defense case is weak, so the defense must rely on these distractions and technicalities to help their case.

Were we too hasty? Did we hire the wrong lawyers?

Now only the verdict of the jury can answer his questions.

As Alex drives home for the day, he thinks about the dinner Hilda has promised him this evening: *pannukakku*, or baked Finnish pancake. This is one of Alex's favorite meals. It is simple, nutritious, and delicious! Hot out of the oven, sprinkled with sugar, rolled up, and eaten with the fingers with a hot cup of coffee and maybe with a few slices of bacon on the side. He cannot wait to get home because this meal will satisfy and relax him.

Alex describes the court happenings for the day when he gets home. He also expresses his concerns regarding Burritt's defense. After a long discussion, Hilda says she is also concerned. But her concern is focused on tomorrow, when she will be called to testify by the prosecution. She is not looking forward to the experience.

Alex tries to ease her anxiety, but he doesn't get far.

Hilda says, "This is like preparing to have surgery tomorrow. You hope and pray that all will go well. But any errors can have profound consequences. I love my brother John, and I don't want to say anything which might jeopardize a verdict of not guilty. But a slip of the tongue could be followed by more questions, which are followed by still more questions." All of Alex's assurances seem to have negligible effect on Hilda. But his simple words, "I love you!", followed by a long hug seem to return a more positive outlook to his wife.

In the morning, as they drive to the courthouse, Alex tries to keep the conversation focused on the things most important to Hilda: her children. It's a successful strategy until they enter the courthouse parking area. Hilda then shuts her eyes in prayer. Alex says, "It will be over soon. I'm sure you'll do fine. William and Barney will be able to explain to the jury any issues which might come up." Using the Burritts as backup settles Hilda's nerves.

TESTIMONY OF ALINA OLLIE

As court opens for the day, Alina Ollie, William Ollie's wife and John's sister, is called by Mr. Galbraith. She provides more details on the times of the day when Bill and John went hunting around 8:00 a.m., came home a little past noon, etc. and corroborates the accuracy of the testimony of her husband.

Hilda is nervous because she doesn't want to be on the witness stand. But Mr. Galbraith calls her next.

TESTIMONY OF MRS. HILDA OLSON THROUGH AN INTERPRETER

Mr. Galbraith asks, "You are the wife of Alex Olson?"

"Yes, sir."

"You live on the Canal Road beyond where your father lived?"

"Yes, sir."

"And how long have you lived there?"

"We moved on May 12 last year from Hancock."

"When did you first hear that your father was killed?"

"Sunday, September 6, in the forenoon."

"How did you hear of his death?"

"My brother, Herbert, came to our place to tell us."

"What time did Herbert come to your place?"

"About six a.m."

"When he came, did he talk to you?"

"Yes. He said Father was sick."

"And what did your husband then do?"

"He went to Father's house with Herbie. They told Alex what happened, but they didn't tell me."

"Do you know why your brother John first left home?"

"I think he went away to earn some money for clothes."

"Did you ever hear John talk about his father?"

"Yes."

"Whatever he said was always kind and friendly towards his father?"

"Yes, never anything bad."

"Your witness, Mr. Burritt."

When Hilda hears Galbraith say those words, she thinks, *Well, that wasn't too bad. And I'm sure Mr. Burritt won't put me on the spot.*

CROSS-EXAMINATION BY MR. BURRITT

"How long did you live in Hancock, Mrs. Olson?"

"Four years."

"Did you visit your father and mother at the Canal when you lived in Hancock?"

"Always, when I had the opportunity."

"When you visited, did you see John there?"

"Yes, when he was home."

"Before this trial started and you heard what some of these witnesses said about what John said to your father, had you ever heard of John making any threats or using any vile language concerning his father?"

"Never."

"And Elizabeth Olson is your husband Alex's sister?"

"Yes, sir."

"Since the fourth day of September last, have you had any conversation with Elizabeth Olson concerning her statement that she thought she saw John Lahnala in the Gekas' Candy Kitchen on the night of September fourth?"

"Yes."

"When was it you had the talk with her?"

"September eighth."

"Now, what did she say concerning it?"

"She said several of them were sitting in the Candy Kitchen at a table, eating ice cream. Selma Hermanson said, 'Look, there is John.' Elizabeth said she looked into a mirror, and a man looked towards them. The man looked like a stranger but didn't say hello. Elizabeth said, 'If he had said something, we would be positive, but he didn't say anything. We thought it was him, but we can't swear to it.' On the ninth, they still said they thought it was him, but said they dare not take an oath on it."

"Said what?"

"They thought it was him but dare not take an oath on it."

"Who are 'they'?"

"Elizabeth and Hilja."

"And they are both sisters of your husband?"

"Yes."

"And what did Hilja say about whether she would take an oath on it being John?"

"She said that she wouldn't dare to take an oath on it."

"When was it you heard Hilja say that?"

"On September eighth and ninth, and after that."

Burritt says, "Thank you, Mrs. Olson. I have no more questions of this witness."

Hilda breathes a sigh of relief as Judge O'Brien says she is excused.

As Hilda walks back to her seat next to Alex, she looks at him. He is smiling his approval. When she sits, Alex gives her a hug and whispers, "Well done!"

Hilda exhales quietly. "That wasn't nearly as bad as I thought it would be."

Mr. Galbraith says, "Your Honor, the People rest."

Judge O'Brien says, "Thank you, Mr. Galbraith."

Chapter 18
Defense Opening Statement

The Court asks, "Mr. Burritt, are you ready with your opening statement?"

William Burritt responds, "Yes, Your Honor."

Looking at the jury, Burritt continues, "Now, gentlemen of the jury, we have consumed several days' time in this case taking the testimony of the witnesses for the purpose of determining whether this boy is guilty of the crime charged against him. He is charged with murdering his father, and the People come into this court seeking to make a case based on circumstantial evidence. Every syllable of it is circumstantial. You have heard a definition of circumstantial evidence and how every link of evidence in the chain of evidence must point to the guilt of the defendant. If any of you have a reasonable doubt, or if any of the evidence doesn't point toward his guilt, you must find the defendant not guilty of this crime. That's the law.

"The theory of the prosecution is that John Lahnala was in the Copper Country on September 4 and 5. But there isn't one iota of evidence which shows that he was in the area. This boy was in the southern part of the Upper Peninsula near Rumley. The People must prove to your satisfaction that he came to Houghton. There is not a syllable of testimony to show that he came to Houghton, not one syllable, except the witnesses who testified that *they think* they saw him in Gekas' Candy Kitchen. However, to find John guilty, *you* must be certain that these witnesses *are not mistaken.* We will show you that these witnesses *are mistaken.*

"The evidence and testimony introduced by the prosecution shows the inconsistency of their theory because no witnesses saw John while he traveling to Houghton, or when he hiked from Houghton to his father's home to supposedly murder him, or when he hiked back to Houghton, or when he was on the train back to Rumley. This is the case the prosecution submits and, upon which they say, 'we rest, and we ask the jury to find this boy guilty of murder.'

"I ask you, if a man is trying to remain hidden from view, as the prosecution contends, why would he voluntarily appear in such a public place as at the Candy Kitchen? Does that make sense to you?

"Now, gentlemen of the jury, I will tell you what we are going to prove. We are going to prove that John and his brother Bill were in the southern part of the Upper Peninsula, more than one hundred miles away from here. They went looking for work on Thursday, September 3.

John met the railroad section man on September 3 and stayed with the section man at his home in Old Swanzy that night. The next morning, September 4, they went out, got boozy, and went back to the section man's house for noon lunch. After lunch, John went to New Swanzy, got a bottle to drink, walked toward Little Lake, and he lay down in a field. It got dark, John drank the rest of his bottle and stayed the rest of the night. That was the night of Friday, September 4.

"John woke about 6:00 a.m. on September 5 and continued to Little Lake. When he got there, he went to a saloon, got a drink, and stayed in some jack pines until around noon. Then he went to Goodman's Store in Little Lake, bought some sardines and a box of crackers, went back into the pines, ate his lunch, and waited for the train to Rumley. He got on that train to go to his brother Bill's house and got off the train at Ferguson. It's a walk of some three-and-a-half miles to Bill's. When he got there, sometime between eight and nine p.m., he rapped on the door, Bill let him in and made a bed for John on the floor, and John spent the night on Bill's floor. That was Saturday night, September 5.

"They all got up on Sunday morning, had a little breakfast, John and Bill took their rifles, went to Ollie's house, and went hunting. They hunted until about noon, went back to Ollie's house, then went back to Bill's and had a meal. They went back into the woods to collect moss for chinking Ollie's house and were in the woods for an hour or so. They went hunting again, shot a deer, and John stayed at Bill's place that Sunday night, September 6.

"On Monday, September 7, John and Bill again went in search of work. When they got back to Bill's place later that day, a telegram told them their father was dead. Both boys cried. Then they went to William Ollie's place to tell them of the death and to make plans to attend the funeral.

"Tuesday morning, September 8, they set out to come to the funeral. They met Mr. Lucas on the train. Lucas had a talk with Bill and John and arrested John before the train got to Houghton. Bill and John both made statements after they got to Houghton. But Mr. Lucas did not take any notes of what John said on the train and didn't get all the facts from John.

"We will introduce testimony by good witnesses to show that this boy was in Little Lake on Saturday, September 5, between twelve and one o'clock p.m., so he could not have been in the Houghton area.

"Mr. Goodman will testify that John bought sardines and crackers at his store and will fix the time. Mr. Goodman has no interest in this case except to see that justice is done.

"Now, the evidence shows that John was born out here at Oskar and that he lived there with his father all his life. There isn't any testimony in this case, gentlemen of the jury, which is worth considering that tends to show there was any ill feeling between the boy and his father.

"As has happened with many boys, John became dissatisfied, he didn't think he was getting enough money, he was getting to be a young man, and he didn't think his clothing was suitable. He wanted something better, so he made up his mind to go out to earn his own living.

"Maybe his father regretted him going, but John went, as thousands of boys have gone, and left their homes under similar circumstances with no particular feeling of ill will existing between him and his father. He went away, but he promised his father that he would come back to help with the haying. And he did so. Then he went away again.

"Now, gentlemen, I have not stated every little fact of the case, but I have stated to you generally what the evidence will be on the part of the defense. We shall introduce testimony showing that these witnesses who claim they saw John in the candy store were mistaken and that their testimony, if it had any value, really has no value.

"We will also show you and introduce evidence that there was someone who was an enemy, or more than one enemy, of August Lahnala. August lived in fear of them. There will be evidence introduced to show that there are other theories that were worthy of investigation other than the theory that the defendant committed this crime. But the officers of the law gave these theories little or no attention. That shows the lack of a thorough investigation.

"We expect that when this case is ended that you will find this boy is not guilty and that you are perfectly satisfied with this boy's innocence.

"Thank you, gentlemen."

The Court says, "Thank you, Mr. Burritt. Please call your first witness."

Chapter 19
Mikkinen, Wayrynen, Walitalo Testimony

TESTIMONY OF ANSOLEM MIKKINEN

Mr. Burritt calls Ansolem Mikkinen as his first witness. "Your name is Ansolem Mikkinen?"

"Yes."

"Where do you live?"

"Oskar."

"Are you acquainted with Fred Johnson?"

"Yes."

"Have you had a discussion with Mr. Johnson since September fifth last?"

"I have."

"Now, during that conversation did he make any statement concerning what he saw or thought he saw in Gekas' Candy Kitchen on the night of September 4 last?"

"Yes, he said that he thought he saw John, but he could not swear to it."

"And state to the jury why he said he wouldn't swear to it."

"He said that he didn't know positively that it was John, and for that reason he wasn't going to swear to it."

CROSS-EXAMINATION BY MR. GALBRAITH

Galbraith asks, "When was it when you had this talk with Fred Johnson?"

"It was the Sunday evening after Lahnala was killed."

"Where were you when that was said?"

"At Johnson's house."

"Who else was present?"

"Alex Lahti, and his hired man."

"Did he say where he thought he had seen John?"

"In the candy store."

"Did he say what John was doing?"

"He said that John was sitting there when he walked in and then John walked out."

"Did Fred say who was with him? That is, who else was with Fred?"

"I think he said two girls, but I don't remember who he said they were."

"But you are sure that Fred said he thought John Lahnala was sitting there and then John got up and walked out."

"Yes."

"And did Fred say why he couldn't swear that this party was John?"

"He said it was many years since he had seen him and never had talked to him."

"Have you talked with anybody since you heard Fred talk about this on the Sunday after August Lahnala's death?"

"I probably talked about it out at the Canal, but I don't remember who I talked to."

REDIRECT EXAMINATION BY MR. BURRITT, JR.

"I will ask you if Mr. Johnson said in your presence that he hadn't conversed with, talked to, John Lahnala?"

"Yes, that's what Fred said."

"And he said when he went into the candy store, that he thought John Lahnala was sitting in the store. Is that what he said?"

"Yes."

"And when he, Johnson, went into the store, the man he thought was John got up and walked out?"

"Yes."

"And that he wasn't sure that it was John. That he wouldn't swear to it?"

"Yes."

TESTIMONY OF MRS. MATILDA WAYRYNEN THROUGH AN INTERPRETER

Mr. Burritt asks, "What is your full name, Mrs. Wayrynen?"

"Matilda Gustava Wayrynen."

"Are you acquainted with Hilja Olson?"

"Yes. I have known her since she was a week old."

"Have you met and talked with Hilja Olson since the fifth day of September last?"

"Yes."

"During any talks that you had with her, state whether or not she said anything concerning seeing John Lahnala in the candy store in Houghton on the night of September 4 last?"

"I asked her if it was John Lahnala who was in the candy kitchen, and she said it looked like John."

"State what else she said."

"She said she wouldn't go and swear to it because he didn't talk to them, but it might have been him."

Burritt says, "Your witness, Mr. Galbraith."

Mr. Galbraith responds, "No questions, Your Honor."

Mrs. Wayrynen is excused.

TESTIMONY OF EVERT WALITALO THROUGH AN INTERPRETER

Mr. Burritt asks, "What is your name?"

"Evert Walitalo."

"Are you acquainted with Elizabeth Olson and Hilja Olson?"

"Yes."

"State whether you have been to their house since the fifth of September last."

"Yes, I have been there."

"Do you remember when it was?"

"Many times. Yesterday was the last time."

"Were you ever there and had a conversation with these girls concerning being in the candy store in Houghton on the fourth of September last?"

"Yes. I remember it was on the ninth of September when there was some talk."

"State what was said by the Olson girls to you or in your presence regarding the night of September 4."

"They said to me that they thought it was John, but they weren't positive."

"They said they thought it was John in the candy store that night, but they were not positive. Is that right?"

"Yes."

"And that was said by both of them?"

"Yes."

CROSS-EXAMINATION BY MR. GALBRAITH

"Where did this discussion take place?"

"At Alex Olson's house."

"And what day was this conversation?"

"On September ninth. The day of the funeral."

"Which of the girls spoke first?"

"I recall Elizabeth spoke first."

"And what did she say?"

"I don't recall exactly what she said but, just as I said a little while ago, that they saw John, but they weren't positive."

"What did Hilja say?"

"She said the same thing."

"And have you talked with others about this conversation?"

"It has been talked about with several people."

Galbraith says, "That's all I have."

Judge O'Brien says, "I believe it's time to adjourn for the day. We will reconvene tomorrow at 9:15 a.m." He pounds the gavel on the sound block, which enhances the sound of the gavel.

Bailiff Trudell says, "All rise," as Judge O'Brien leaves the courtroom.

Chapter 20
John Lahnala Testimony

When the court reconvenes, the courtroom is packed because people want to hear what John Lahnala has to say in his own defense. The prosecuting attorney leans forward in anticipation when Burritt calls for John to take the stand.

Through an interpreter, Mr. Burritt Sr. asks, "What is your name?"

"John Lahnala."

"How old are you, John?"

"Eighteen."

"And what was your father's name?"

"August."

"Did you ever go to school in Oskar?"

"A little bit."

"How far did you live from the school?"

"About a half mile."

"Was the school you went to an English school?"

"Yes."

"Did you learn to read and write English?"

"Not much."

"Now have you learned to read and write in the Finnish language?"

"Yes."

"And how did you learn that?"

"My mother taught me."

"After you got old enough to work, where did you live, and where did you work?"

"At home at first."

"How old was you when you first quit working at home?"

"Sixteen."

"Why did you quit working at home?"

"Pa wouldn't pay me or get me any good clothes."

"Please briefly tell us where you went after you left home."

"Well, first I went to Redridge and worked at the Baltic Mill for about a month. Then I went to the Beacon Hill Mill for three weeks until haying time."

Burritt interrupts, "Did you visit home when you worked away?"

"Yes, many Sundays and sometimes in the evening."

Burritt asks, "And at haying time, what did you do?"

"I went home to help my Pa for about a month. After haying, I went to Minnesota and was there about four months, until I came back here in January 1914."

"Did you stay at home after you returned to this area?"

"No. I stayed at Zurcher's, doing farm work for him for a while. Then in April, I went to Rumley and bought some land close to my brother. I worked and stayed at the lumber camps down there until late August, when I got fired.

"And then what did you do?"

John relates the details of his activities from Wednesday, September 2, until he left with the other family members to come to the funeral on September 8.

After John's narrative, Mr. Burritt says, "Your witness, Mr. Galbraith."

CROSS-EXAMINATION BY MR. GALBRAITH

"When you worked for your father, you worked hard, didn't you?"

"Yes, but he said I wasn't working enough."

"And even though you worked as hard as you could, you couldn't please him, could you?"

"Not always."

"And you didn't have as good clothes as the other boys around Oskar, did you?"

"I had hardly anything to put on."

"And when you would ask your father for clothes, would he give any reason for not giving them to you?"

"No, he didn't give any reason."

"Did he provide your sisters with clothes?"

Mr. Burritt says, "We object to that as immaterial."

Mr. Galbraith replies, "I think, Your Honor, in view of the examination, it's very material."

The Court says, "You may answer."

"No, they didn't have much of anything either."

"Now, how much livestock did your father have the last year you were at home?"

"There must have been about twenty cows, maybe ten of them were milkers, and two horses."

"Who took care of them?"

"I always took care of the cows when I was at home. Pa didn't help much. Ma helped."

"And you didn't have any Sunday clothes, did you?"

"No."

"Now, when you were working at Redridge and Beacon Hill, you came home many Sundays?"

"Yes."

"Do you recall one Sunday when you came home, and your uncle Enoch and his wife were at your father's place?"

"They didn't visit when I was there."

"You are absolutely sure of that?"

"Quite sure, yes."

"And if your aunt Vertriga says she visited there, she is absolutely mistaken?"

"Yes, she's lying."

Ouch! thinks Alex. Alex does not like John calling somebody else a liar. He looks at the jury, and his juror three is pursing his lips and has a steely, speculative frown. Alex thinks that is not a good sign.

"Do you know Eino Torvinen?"

"Yes."

"Did you go hunting with him?"

"Sometimes."

"Do you remember talking with Torvinen about the fact that your father might stop your pay when you were at Redridge or Beacon Hill?"

"No."

"You knew your father could stop your pay because you were underage, didn't you?"

"I heard that he could do that because I was a minor, yes."

"Did you ever talk to someone about what you'd do if your father did stop your pay?"

"I think I talked to another fella at the mill. I think I said if he should stop my pay, I would take clothes from the store."

"Why did you say you'd take clothes from the store?"

"I think the other fella's pay was stopped at one time, so that's what he did."

"You'd steal from the store?"

"No, I'd buy it. Wages was paid through the store. I'd just tell the store to take the money out of my wages."

"I see. While you were making hay at your father's place, did your father have other men working for him besides yourself?"

"Yes."

"Do you know what the going wage was for haymakers in 1914?"

"Two dollars a day and board, I think. About that."

"Did your father pay you for your work while you were making hay?"

"No."

"And you left home again and went to Minnesota. You bought some clothes when you were there?"

"Yes."

"And you came back in January 1914?"

"I believe that's when it was."

"And after you came back, you worked and stayed at Zurcher's?"

"Yes."

"Now, you say you know Hilda Solmonson?"

"Yes, I know her."

"You'd visit with her?"

"We'd sometimes talk."

"And didn't you frequently refer to your father as 'slouch' or 'old slouch'?"

"I don't remember that."

"Did you talk with Hilda about your father being in jail?"

"I don't remember."

"You think, then, that when Hilda says that you spoke about his being in jail, that she's lying about it?"

Mr. Burritt says, "I object to that question as being incompetent."

The Court replies, "Yes, I think I will sustain that objection."

Alex thinks, *Finally, some points for our side!*

"Do you remember the pistol Bill bought?"

"Yes."

"And did you hear Hilda Solmonson's testimony?"

"Yes, most of it."

"And you heard her say you came out of the bedroom at Bill's place with the pistol in your hand and said, 'This is what I will use to bore the old slouch through'?"

"I heard her say so."

"Did you say that?"

"I don't remember that. She must be lying."

Alex says to himself, *There's that 'liar' thought again!* Alex has known young men who cannot seem to tell the truth, even when they're backed into a corner. Some even get hostile in this situation. He doesn't believe this represents John's character, but what does the jury think? Two jurors adjust themselves in their seats, and Alex wonders if they are starting to think that John is lying to try to defend himself. That would not be good.

Galbraith asks John, "Can you tell us what Bill did at Zurcher's?"

"He drove the milk wagon."

"And do you recall that you and Bill and Zurcher were in the milk house one time, and you were talking about your father being in jail?"

"I don't remember."

"Do you recall Mr. Zurcher testifying that at this time you spoke of your father as a 'son of a bitch'?"

"I don't remember that I have said anything like that."

"Are you willing to say on oath now that you did not at that time call your father 'a son of a bitch'?"

"I can't positively remember, but I think that I did not say so."

"Were you pleased your father was in jail?"

"No."

"Did you not say to Miss Solmonson or John Zurcher that you were pleased that your father was in jail?"

"I don't remember."

"Now, you provided quite a bit of detail in response to questions from Mr. Burritt about your whereabouts from September 4 to September 8, 1914, as to where you were and what you did. I ask if there is anything in that testimony which you'd like to change?"

"No, sir. It's all the truth."

Judge O'Brien interrupts Mr. Galbraith's line of questioning, saying, "It's getting rather late in the day. Do you anticipate that you will be questioning this witness much longer?"

"It all depends on the witness's replies to my questions, Your Honor."

O'Brien says, "I understand. Considering the hour, unless counsel has objections, let's adjourn for the day."

Mr. Galbraith and Mr. Burritt both say they have no objections.

Judge O'Brien says, "Court is adjourned until 10:00 a.m. tomorrow."

When court reconvenes the following morning, John Lahnala is still on the witness stand. Judge O'Brien reminds him that he is still under oath.

Mr. Galbraith continues with his questions. "Now, I believe you said on September 8, you all started for the Copper Country for your father's funeral."

"Yes."

"Where did you see Mr. Lucas first?"

"I think it was at the depot in Marquette."

Mr. Galbraith holds the pliers, which are People's Exhibit 8, and asks, "And where did you get these pliers?"

"I didn't get them from anywhere."

"When was the first time you saw these pliers?"

"Down in the sheriff's office."

"When was the last time you used these pliers?"

"I never used them."

Chapter 21
Bernard Goodman Testimony

Mr. Burritt saunters toward the witness stand and asks, "What is your name?"

"Bernard Goodman."

"And what business are you in?"

"In cutting and manufacturing lumber."

"Have you a mill and store?"

"Yes, sir."

"And where are they located?"

"Both are in Little Lake."

"I call your attention, Mr. Goodman, to this defendant, John Lahnala, and I ask you whether you ever saw him before?"

"Yes sir, I have."

"State to the jury the first time you saw him and the circumstances surrounding that time."

"It was on September 5, Saturday morning that I saw him. I was at my store, and I saw a man walk in the front entrance. As he approached, I thought to myself from his appearance, 'Here is another fellow looking for a handout, for something to eat.' As he came in, I said to myself, 'I'll just wait and see what he says.' I kind of let on that I was doing something so that he would talk to the clerk. He stepped up to the counter, and he asked for some crackers, and I heard the papers rattle. Pretty soon, he called for some sardines. I looked and saw the clerk take down a box of sardines, and the man reached into his pocket to pay for it.

"Right away, I said to myself, 'That fellow is no bum.' I looked at him and saw he was a Finlander, and his light hair caught my eye first. I said to myself, 'I might have known better. Those fellows generally have money to pay for what they get.' After he paid for his crackers and sardines, he turned to walk out. I said to the clerk, 'He may have seen better days, but he has got money to pay for what he got. I said he looks as if he may have been out for a good time and has a ragged edge.' The clerk said, 'By gosh, he does, but he has got the money to pay for his goods.' As we watched him, he turned out of view."

"And what time of day was that?"

"As I remember, about two o'clock."

"And do you remember the day of the month?"

"Yes. It was Saturday, September 5."

"Last year, 1914?"

"Yes, sir."

"And how are you so sure of the date?"

"The principal reason I am sure is that the Little Lake Lumber Company, of which I am general manager, had a note due on the fifth of September. I intended to pay it, but I wasn't able to. I had to renew the note. I mailed it that morning on the seven-thirty train that goes to Marquette. That's why I am positive of the date."

"Did you notice how Mr. Lahnala was dressed?"

"He had on a pair of faded yellow pants, a belt, and a shirt that was dirty. He was very unkempt looking, looked as though he had been laying around."

"I call the witness's attention to a pair of yellow overalls and a belt. I ask whether they are the ones the defendant had on."

"Well, sir, they look just about like the pants he had on, alright. The belt too."

"And you have a mill close to the store?"

"Yes sir, about five hundred feet away."

"And was it running that Saturday?"

"No, sir. We quit sawing on the afternoon of the third."

"Now, on what side of the store is the counter where this fellow you saw bought the sardines?"

"On the right as you come in."

"Now, when was the next time that you saw this defendant after seeing him on September fifth?"

"Why, when I saw him here at the courthouse."

"State whether you recognized him when you saw him here."

"I recognized him right away."

"State whether or not you are certain he is the man who came to your store and bought the sardines."

"I am positive he is the man who bought the sardines on September fifth."

"Now, in going from your mill to the jack pines near the mill, state whether there were slab piles through the yard."

"That's where we had our woodyard. We dumped our slabs and piled them there."

"And if a person would walk from the jack pines to go to the saloon or depot, would he go close to the mill?"

"Yes, he would pass pretty close to the mill."

CROSS-EXAMINATION BY MR. GALBRAITH

"When did you start operating at Little Lake?"

"In the fall of 1908."

"And last September fifth, you say you were in your store at Little Lake, but you didn't wait on this man?"

"That's correct. My clerk, Joe Robarge, waited on him."

"And where is Joe Robarge?"

"This winter he is foreman on our landing at Stella, on the Munising Railway."

"And when you first saw this man, you thought he was looking for a handout, so you gave the clerk a chance to handle him?"

"Yes, sir."

"And how far were you from this man at that time?"

"About from here to the stenographer."

"And you saw him buy crackers and sardines?"

"Yes sir. He bought the cheapest sardines we had. It struck me he was looking for quantity, not quality."

"How much is that can of sardines?"

"That's a ten cent can."

"And this fellow had on the faded trousers which have been offered in evidence and the belt, is that right?"

"It looks like the pants, but many belts look like that, so I can't be sure of that."

"And the coat he's now wearing?"

"It looks like the same coat, maybe a little lighter in color."

"And you know or see a great many Finns, do you not?"

"Yes, sir."

"And light hair is one of the distinguishing characteristics of the nationality, is it not?"

"Yes, sir."

"And this party that you saw was a light-haired Finn?"

"Yes, sir."

"And did you get a look at his shoes?"

"Not a good look. Just that they weren't new. I know that."

"Pretty well worn?"

"They looked to be."

"Anything on his head?"

"I think it was a slouchy hat."

"And how long was this man in the store?"

"Just long enough to buy the crackers and sardines and go out. About three minutes."

REDIRECT EXAMINATION BY MR. BURRITT

"Now, you say you are positive of the date because of the note you had to renew."

"Yes, sir."

"Where is the note?"

"In my pocket."

"Produce it, please."

"Here it is."

Burritt asks the Court, "May I have this note marked as an exhibit in this case?"

The Court responds, "Certainly."

"Now, I call the witness's attention to this note and ask if this is the note you had as a renewal note on that date, September 5, 1914?"

"It is."

Galbraith says, "I object to this as incompetent and ask the answer to be stricken. It's merely a self-serving declaration, seeking to corroborate his testimony."

Burritt responds, "It's perfectly competent."

The Court rules, "I think that would be competent as fixing the date, and I will let the answer stand."

Alex agrees, nods his head, and thinks, *Makes sense to me, too! Thank you, Judge.*

Burritt says, "We offer this exhibit in evidence."

Galbraith says, "I object to that, Your Honor, as incompetent, something entirely immaterial and irrelevant in the record. Its only purpose can be to corroborate."

The Court replies, "I think I will admit it."

Burritt says, "I pass this note to the jury for their examination."

He then says, "And the fellow, when he came into your store that day, did he look as though he had been laying out, maybe been drinking?"

"Yes, very much so."

RECROSS-EXAMINATION BY MR. GALBRAITH

"And are you positive that the clerk, Joe Robarge, waited on the man who came into your store that day?"

"I am positive."

"Just as positive as everything else you said?"

"No, sir. I am dead positive it was September the fifth, and I am positive it was a Finlander with light hair that bought the lunch. That fellow there, that's the guy. And I am positive Joe Robarge waited on him."

"And there can't be any mistake that this is the man?"

"Not when I look at the fellow there. He's the fellow that came in the store; I stake my life on it."

"No more questions."

Chapter 22
Paul Johnson Testimony

Mr. Burritt Sr. calls Paul Johnson to testify. He asks, "Where do you live, Mr. Johnson?"

"Little Lake."

"Please state to the jury where you were on September 5, 1914."

"In B. J. Goodman's mill at Little Lake."

"I ask you if the mill was running that day?"

"It was not."

"And what were you doing on September 5?"

"I was whitewashing in the morning and doing some repairs on the whitewash machine in the afternoon."

"Now, I will ask you, while you were working there if you saw anyone pass by the mill that day?"

"I did."

"What time of day was that?"

"Around two o'clock in the afternoon."

"And what direction was this person coming from?"

"From the direction of the store."

"How far away were you from the person who passed the mill at that time?"

"About twenty-five or thirty feet."

"How long did you observe this person?"

"About five minutes."

"I will ask you if you have ever seen this defendant, John Lahnala, before?"

"Not until that day."

Pointing at John, Burritt asks, "Is this the person you saw pass near the mill that day, September 5?"

"Yes, sir."

"And in which direction did he go when you saw him at the mill?"

"He was going away from the mill, through the yard, toward the slab piles and jack pines."

"How do you know it was September 5?"

"The mill shut down on September third, on the fourth we swept up, and on the fifth, we were going to whitewash."

"And do these look like the trousers the person wore when he passed by the mill?"

"Yes, sir."

"And his coat?"

"It looks like the same coat."

"And are you positive that this was the man you saw pass by the mill on September 5 in the afternoon?"

"Yes, sir."

CROSS-EXAMINATION BY MR. GALBRAITH

"You say in the afternoon of September 5 you were repairing a whitewash machine."

"Yes, sir."

"And how long did you follow the man with your eyes?"

"About four or five minutes."

"How far did he walk in that time?"

"About three or four hundred feet, I should say."

"Then most of the time, his back was toward you?"

"Yes, sir."

"Had you ever seen him before?"

"No, sir."

"You didn't see where he was going?"

"No, sir."

"Wasn't carrying anything in his hands?"

"He might have carried something in his left hand, not in his right."

"And did Mr. Barney Burritt come down to Little Lake?"

"Yes, sir."

"Did you meet with Mr. Burritt?"

"Yes."

"What did he say to you?"

"He asked if I saw anybody at the mill."

"And what did you say?"

"I said I saw several men."

"And then Mr. Burritt described the man to you and asked you if you had seen him walking past?"

"Yes."

"How many men did you see walking past the mill on September 5?"

"Just the one man."

"Do you know Mr. B. J. Goodman?"

"Yes, sir."

"And when you traveled from Little Lake up here, were you on the same coach as Mr. Goodman?"

"Well, for about five or ten minutes we were in the same coach."

"You have been together somewhat up here?"

"Somewhat around town."

"And the two of you never talked about being witnesses here?"

"No, sir."

"You never knew you were to be witnesses in the same case?"

"We knew we were both witnesses. We were both subpoenaed."

"And you never asked him for a description of the fellow you had seen?"

"No, sir."

"And you don't know whether this is the same party or whether it's somebody that looked somewhat like him?"

"It looks exactly like him."

"And it may be some other fellow that looks like the party that you saw."

"It might have been his twin brother."

"I am asking for a serious answer. You are under oath, aren't you?"

"Yes, sir."

"And you understand the nature of an oath?"

"Yes, sir."

"And the penalty?"

"Yes, sir."

"Now seriously, we want to know whether you are prepared to swear that this is the man."

"In my own thoughts, I do."

"But it may be somebody that looks like that party, the party that you saw may be somebody that looks like this man."

"It might. The exact picture of him."

"And when you saw him near the mill, you thought he was another bum?"

"Yes, sir."

REDIRECT EXAMINATION BY BARNEY BURRITT

Barney Burritt says, "I will ask you, Mr. Johnson, if from where you were when you saw this defendant, you had a perfectly plain view of him when he was going through the mill?"

"Yes, sir."

"And you watched him until he got out of sight."

"Yes, sir."

"And where did he walk before he disappeared from your view?"

"Past some slab piles and into the jack pines."

"Do you know whether these are the identical trousers he had on, or are they similar-looking trousers you saw that day?"

"They look exactly as he had on."

"And I will ask you if I described this defendant to you *before* I asked you if anyone passed through there that day, or if you noticed anyone that day?"

"You did not."

"And what did you tell me before I described anyone to you?"

"I said there was a man I seen around there that day."

"And I ask you if you didn't describe this person to me that you saw there before?"

"Yes, I did, sir."

"And I ask if you didn't describe him just as you have described him here?"

"Yes, sir."

"And after it was all over, I ask if I didn't show you a picture of this defendant?"

"Just his head and shoulders."

"And I will ask you if you said that was the man?"

"Yes, sir."

Chapter 23
John Lahnala Recalled

Mr. Galbraith asks the Court, "Your Honor, I would like to recall John Lahnala for a few follow-up questions, if I may."

Judge O'Brien says, "I think that would be alright."

As John starts to walk to the witness stand, the Court says to John, "You understand that you are still under oath?"

John responds, "Yes, sir."

Galbraith says, "You heard the testimony of Mr. Goodman?"

"Yes."

"And you understood it all?"

"Almost."

"And you heard the testimony of Mr. Johnson?"

"Yes."

"And you understood it?"

"Yes."

"Why don't you take the questions and give answers in English, rather than through an interpreter?"

"I can't answer your questions correctly."

"You can understand them correctly?"

"Almost all."

Galbraith says, "I insist, your Honor, hereafter this witness shall at least take the questions direct."

The Court says, "We can try it."

Galbraith says, "On Monday morning, you and Bill started out for work?"

No answer from Mr. Lahnala.

The Court asks, "Did you understand the question?"

"Not all."

Mr. Galbraith repeats the question, this time more slowly. "Monday morning, September 7, you and Bill started out looking for work?"

"Yes."

"Now, did you tell Mr. Lucas or Mr. Heikkila that you got whiskey in a saloon on Saturday morning?"

"Yes."

"Did you tell Mr. Heikkila and Mr. Lucas that you went into the jack pines and slept until noon?"

"Yes."

"And did you tell Mr. Heikkila and Mr. Lucas that you went into a store and got a lunch at noon?"

"No."

"Why didn't you tell them that?"

"They didn't ask me."

"Did you tell them that you went back into the saloon after you had your dinner and got a glass of beer?"

"I can't remember if they asked me."

"Did you tell them?"

"I only told them what they asked me about."

"Now, John, isn't it true that they asked you to tell them what you did on that Saturday?"

"Not Saturday. I answered just what they asked me. I didn't talk nothing more."

"When you talked, it was only in answer to questions?"

"Yes."

"Did you tell them what you did at noon?"

"I don't understand you."

"What about it don't you understand?"

"I don't know what you mean with that word."

"Did you—do you understand that?"

"Yes."

"Tell—"

"Yes."

"Them—"

"Yes."

"What—"

"Yes."

"You—"

"Yes."

"Did—"

"Yes."

"At—"

"Yes."

"Noon?"

William Burritt says, "We can't continue like this. How can we get the truth if the witness don't understand the question? It's important for him to understand what he's asked."

The Court says, "We'll continue to use the interpreter."

The interpreter is used again for questions and answers. The interpreter states the question in Finnish for John.

"Yes, I told them I went to sleep."

"And when did you buy this gun from Bill?"

"I can't remember what month it was."

"When was the last time you saw this pistol before it was brought to this courtroom?"

"I can't remember. I think when I gave it to my brother to put away."

"When was that?"

"Early July."

"Did you ever carry this gun when you were hunting?"

"Not that I can remember."

"Did you see Fred Johnson, Selma Hermanson, and Elizabeth and Hilja Olson at Gekas' Candy Kitchen the evening of September fourth last?"

"No. I was in Rumley."

"Did you, with that pistol, on the evening of last September fifth, shoot your father in his kitchen?"

"I did not."

REDIRECT EXAMINATION BY MR. BURRITT

"Now, John, do you know where the Gekas' Candy Kitchen is in Houghton?"

"No."

"Do you remember whether you have ever been there or not?"

"I think I have never been there."

"And you remember when you was on the way to your father's funeral that the officers questioned you and put you under arrest?"

"Yes."

"And at that time state whether, so far as they asked you questions, you told them the truth."

"Yes."

"And did they ask you as many questions as you have been asked here on the witness stand?"

"No."

"If they had, would you have told them the same as you have testified here?"

"Yes."

Changing topics, Burritt asks, "How did you carry the sardines and crackers while you were going from the store to the jack pines?"

"I put them in the pockets of my coat."

"And state whether you put your coat on when you left the store or before that time, before you got to the jack pines."

"When I got out of the store, I put it on."

"Now, about the trousers. State whether you wore those trousers on the second through the fifth of last September on the trips you have testified that you made."

"I was wearing them."

"And you had them on when you went to Goodman's store to buy crackers and sardines?"

"Yes."

"And what coat did you have on, John, when you made that trip?"

"This coat. The one I now have on."

"What have you had done with that coat since Saturday, September 5?"

"My brother's wife cleaned it."

"When was that?"

"September 6."

"I call the witness's attention to this pair of pliers marked Exhibit 8. I ask you, John, whether you have ever seen these pliers before and, if so, when and where."

"I saw them at the sheriff's office after I had been arrested."

"Was that the first time you had seen these pliers?"

"Yes."

"The officers didn't show you these pliers when they questioned you, did they?"

"No."

"Did your brother have pliers like this at his house in Rumley?"

"He had another kind."

"Now, why didn't you tell the officers everything that you have told here when they talked to you?"

"Because they didn't ask me. When I was going to say something, they would stop me."

"Who stopped you?"

"I don't know who it was."

"Well, what would he say to you?"

"I think he said, 'Answer to what you are asked.'"

"And did you do as you were bidden to do?"

"Yes."

Mr. Burritt continues, "Now John, do you know anything about who killed your father?"

"I do not."

"No further questions."

Judge O'Brien says, "You may step down." He adds, "We accomplished much this week, but it's getting late. Let's adjourn for the weekend. Court will reconvene on Monday, March 1 at 10 a.m."

After court adjourned, Alex wanted to talk to John. He went to the county jail to congratulate John on his good testimony, saying in Finn, "I think you did really well on the stand today, John!"

John says, "Thanks. But I get embarrassed when I must talk in Finn. I'm old enough to be able to defend myself in English. But I can't understand English good enough to do it! Ma was right when she told me I should take my English schooling more seriously."

Alex replies, "Many people in the Oskar area cannot speak English as well as you can, John."

"There are many words I cannot understand. Sometimes I ask people to explain what they mean when I don't understand. They try to explain what they mean, but I don't even understand the words they use to explain! Can you understand how that makes me feel, Alex?"

"Yes, and I can see that it frustrates you. You'll have opportunities to practice your English when this trial is over. But please don't lose focus. What's important now is that you did a good job today defending yourself."

"Thank you, Alex. Maybe you can help me with my English when this is all over?"

"Of course. I'll be pleased to work with you on your English!"

“How do you think the trial is going?” John asked.

“Overall, I think it’s going good. Do you mind if I make a suggestion?”

“Of course not! If it will help me, I’ll take whatever advice you want to give me.”

“Alright. I watched the jury closely today, and I think they want to believe you. However, if you are on the witness stand again, use your words carefully. When you testified that your aunt Vertriga and Hilda Solmonson must be lying about your interactions with your Pa, it looked like a couple of jury members didn’t believe you. Hilda and your aunt don’t have much reason to lie, because they have little to gain by lying. But they might think that you will lie to defend yourself.”

“I never thought of that!” said John. “I wish I could take those words back.”

“Well, don’t worry about it, John. Your lawyers are doing a good job, and if they thought it was much to worry about, they’d be talking with you about it.”

After giving John some bits of news from home, Alex and John say their goodbyes, and Alex heads home.

Chapter 24
Bill and Hannah Lahnala Testimony

TESTIMONY OF BILL LAHNALA

On Monday, Mr. Burritt continues his defense interrogation, calling Bill Lahnala to the stand. After Mr. Lahnala is sworn, Burritt asks, "What is your name?"

"Matt William Lahnala."

"And how old are you?"

"Twenty-eight."

"And do most people call you 'Matt'?"

"Most call me 'Bill.'"

"And you are John Lahnala's brother?"

"Yes, sir."

"And do you recognize this pistol?"

"Yes, sir."

"When was the first time you saw it?"

"In Swift's Hardware Store when I went there to buy a pistol."

"When was that?"

"A year ago, in the fall or winter."

"Why did you buy it?"

"I was working for Zurcher, and I had quite a bit of money sometimes to take home."

"Why were you carrying so much money?"

"I was delivering milk and doing collections for Zurcher."

"And you thought you might be robbed?"

"Yes. I bought it during the mining strike. There were many robberies in the area because the pay of the copper miners was stopped when they went on strike. People needed money, so some stole it!"

"This was when the 'Italian Hall Disaster' occurred on Christmas Eve?"

"Yes."

Burritt says, "I can understand your concern. Now, where was this pistol when your father was killed?"

"I had it in my tool chest at home in Rumley. I didn't need it after I moved there."

"And when the sheriff's office asked if they could get into your tool chest, did you give them permission?"

"Yes, sir."

"Gave them permission to get the pistol and anything else they wanted to get there?"

"Yes, sir. They wanted all the pliers I had. I told them they are locked up in my tool chest. I keep them locked because I don't want them laying around anyplace."

"Did you give them the key to the tool chest?"

"Yes, sir."

"I direct your attention to five pairs of pliers. Have you seen these tools before?"

"Yes sir, they are my pliers."

"Where were these tools on September fifth?"

"They were in my tool chest."

"I call the witness's attention to People's Exhibit 8, another pair of pliers. Did you ever see these before?"

"I did."

"Where?"

"In the sheriff's office. Sheriff Cruse showed them to me on September 8."

"Had you ever seen them before?"

"No, never."

"Thank you, Bill."

Mr. Galbraith has no questions.

TESTIMONY OF HANNAH LAHNALA

Before testifying, Mrs. Lahnala says, "I want someone to talk for me."

Mr. Burritt asks, "Can't you talk English, Mrs. Lahnala?"

"I don't think I can talk enough, and I don't understand everything."

"Let's try and see. If you need any assistance, the interpreter will assist you. Your name is what?"

"Hannah Lahnala."

"And you are the wife of Bill Lahnala?"

"Yes, sir."

"Now you've heard the testimony about this pistol?"

"Yes, sir."

"And state where it was kept, if you know."

"Bill kept it in his tool chest first. After that, it was in the drawer of the small dresser."

"And why was it kept there?"

"So I could use it if I needed it."

"And did you see it often?"

"Yes, every time I looked in the drawer."

"You live in the woods?"

"Yes, sir."

"And what kind of animals were around there?"

"They talk about porcupines and wolves and bears."

"Do you know how to shoot this gun?"

"I can shoot with it."

"Have you practiced with it?"

"Yes."

"Do you know when that pistol was first taken out of the dresser drawer where it had been kept?"

"Bill took it out when he shot the cat."

"Why did he shoot the cat?"

"It was sick and dying. He put it out of its misery."

"What did he do with the gun after he shot the cat?"

"He cleaned it and filled it with cartridges and put it back in the drawer."

"In the same drawer?"

"Yes."

"Now, do you know if the gun was in the drawer when John and Bill were away looking for work on the second, third, fourth, and fifth of September?"

"Yes, it was there."

"How do you know it was there?"

"Because I looked so often in that drawer."

"And Monday evening, September 7, you received a telegram?"

"Bill did, yes, sir."

"And what did it say?"

"Come home at once, Father is killed."

"And then what happened?"

"We were going to start for home, but it was too late to get the train. We started the next day."

CROSS-EXAMINATION BY MR. GALBRAITH

"Where are you now living, Mrs. Lahnala?"

"At my mother-in-law's home."

"At Mrs. August Lahnala's?"

"Yes, sir."

"You and Mrs. Lahnala and her children and Bill and your children all living in the same house."

"Yes, sir."

"And that's been true since you came back for the funeral?"

"Yes."

"And your husband, Bill, and John worked together at Zurcher's?"

"Yes, sir."

"And did you hear John and his father talking at all when John worked at Zurcher's?"

"Yes, many times."

"And John often went home and saw your father when he worked there?"

"Yes, many times."

"Now, you say that this pistol was kept in the dresser drawer when you lived at your house in Rumley, is that right?"

"Yes. But Bill locked it in his tool chest when we came here."

"And you swear it was in the dresser drawer on September second and third last year?"

"Yes, it was there."

"And what time of day did you see it on those days?"

"I don't remember."

"What time of day on the fourth was it when you saw it there?"

"I don't remember the time then either, but I can remember that particular day because I was going to oil the sewing machine, and I saw it then."

"And what time on the fifth did you see it?"

"I don't remember that."

"Was it just lying there, or did it have a case on it?"

"It was just lying there and fully loaded."

"Did John and Bill shoot this gun?"

"Yes."

"And you shot it too?"

"Yes. They were teasing me that I would be afraid to shoot with it, and I took it and shot at a tree."

"How many times did you shoot?"

"Several times."

Galbraith says, "No more questions." and Hannah Lahnala is excused.

Chapter 25
John Lehto and Barney Burritt Testimony

Mr. Burritt asks John Lehto, "Where do you live, Mr. Lehto?"

"I live in Hancock."

"Was you acquainted with August Lahnala?"

"Yes, well acquainted."

"When you were living in Hancock, did he ever stay overnight at your place?"

Mr. Galbraith says, "I object to that as indefinite. The time span could be many years."

Mr. Burritt says, "I am going to show when it was, if he ever did."

The Court says, "I think I will let him answer."

"I am not sure whether he spent the night or not, but he asked me to let him in one night to stay all night."

"I would like to ask the question again. Did you let him in, and did he stay all night?"

"He came to my bar, and I gave him accommodations. We have some rooms upstairs of the bar. But I don't know if he stayed all night or not. There was an old man taking care of that."

"When was that?"

"It was a little more than a year ago."

"What reason did he give for wanting to stay there all night?"

"He said he was afraid to go home, afraid someone would kill him."

"What condition was Mr. Lahnala in? Whether he was intoxicated or not."

"I couldn't say he was drunk exactly, but one could see that he had been drinking."

CROSS-EXAMINATION BY MR. GALBRAITH

"What time was it that he came to your bar and spoke to you?"

"It was close to eleven o'clock. It was quite late."

"And it was plain to be seen that he had been drinking?"

"Yes, a little, but he wasn't drunk at all."

TESTIMONY OF B. H. T. BURRITT

William Burritt calls his son, Barney, to the witness stand and asks, "Are you one of the attorneys for the defendant?"

"I am."

"Now, did you go to Little Lake for the purpose of making some investigation last fall?"

"I did."

"And who did you see?"

"I saw Mr. Bernard Goodman, Mr. Steele, and Mr. Johnson."

"Did you go to Goodman's store?"

"I did."

"What sent you to Goodman's store?"

"I went there to see whether this defendant was there on Saturday, September 5 last."

"And did you show these gentlemen a photo of this defendant taken last November 12?"

"I did."

"How did it happen that you went directly to Goodman's store when you went to Little Lake?"

"I went directly there because John Lahnala told us that he bought crackers and sardines in Goodman's store on Saturday the fifth of September in the afternoon."

Burritt says, "Thank you. I have no further questions of this witness. Mr. Galbraith?"

Mr. Galbraith says, "I have no questions."

Mr. Burritt declares, "Your Honor, the defense rests."

Mr. Galbraith says, "Your Honor, in rebuttal, I would like to call Mr. Frank Steele."

Chapter 26
Frank Steele Testimony

Frank Steele, a witness produced and sworn on behalf of the People, examined in chief by Mr. Galbraith, testifies as follows.

"What is your name?"

"Franklin Steele."

"And where do you live?"

"Little Lake."

"What is your occupation there?"

"Inspecting lumber and yard foreman for Little Lake Lumber Company."

"Who kept the time at the yard at Little Lake Lumber Company?"

"I kept the time, marked it in the books."

"That was part of your responsibility during August and September last?"

"Yes, sir."

"And where is the book kept where you keep the time?"

"In the office."

Mr. Galbraith says, "I would offer for identification a book and ask it be marked People's Exhibit 17."

Mr. Burritt says, "No objection."

Mr. Galbraith continues, "I show you this book, which has been marked People's Exhibit 17. I ask you what it is."

Mr. Steele replies, "It is the time book for the lumber company."

"Directing your attention to page 22 and the words across the top 'Time book for the month of September 1914', have you seen this page before?"

"Yes, sir."

"And what are the markings, the numbers 1 through 31 running across the top of the page?"

"They are the days of the month."

"And the names in the first column on the left are the names of the employees?"

"Yes, sir."

"And these pencil markings to the right of the name of "Paul Johnson," are they in your hand?"

Burritt says, "I object, Your Honor, to the use of this book and to the markings in the book as incompetent and immaterial. And the markings and the dates and names are hearsay in part. May I ask the witness one question?"

The Court says, "Certainly."

Burritt asks, "Did you make these entries yourself, Mr. Steele?"

"I wouldn't swear to all of them. I will swear to those that I made."

Burritt says, "Then we object to the question for the further reason that the witness's testimony as to the contents of the book would be hearsay in part."

The Court says, "I will overrule the particular objection and let the witness testify to the entries that he has made."

Burritt says, "Note an exception."

Galbraith continues, "I call your attention to the name of Paul Johnson and to the pencil markings in the squares to the right of his name and ask if any of those markings are in your hand?"

"Yes, sir."

"How many of the markings are in your hand?"

"All except the twenty-sixth, twenty-seventh, and twenty-eighth of the month."

Galbraith asks, "To the right of the name of Paul Johnson and under column marked 1 is the number ten. What does that number indicate, Mr. Steele?"

"That's the number of hours he worked that day."

"Now, using the book to refresh your memory, how many hours did Mr. Johnson work on September 5, 1914?"

"On the fifth, he worked ten hours."

"I call your attention to a mark above the hours he worked on the fifth and ask what that mark indicates?"

"That mark above the 10 represents work done at the farm."

"Can you explain that please?"

"Well, you see, Mr. Goodman has a farm near Little Lake, and when things are slow at the mill, he sometimes has his workers do some work at his farm."

"So, if he worked at the mill on September 5, there would be no mark above the hours he worked. Is that correct?"

Burritt says, "I object to the question as hearsay."

The Court says, "Take the answer."

"Yes sir. There would be no mark."

"And you yourself took the time of the men who worked in the mill and the mill yard, did you not?"

"Yes, sir, I did."

"Referring to the book, and according to the book, where was Paul

Johnson on September 5 last?"

"He worked at the farm."

CROSS-EXAMINATION BY MR. BURRITT

"You said you were the timekeeper for Goodman's, and you recorded the hours a man worked and where he worked?"

"Yes, sir."

"I ask you if you kept that from your knowledge, as you supposed the fact to be?"

"I put down the number of hours each day regardless of —"

"Will you answer my question? I say you kept the time, made the entry as you believed at that time, as to the number of hours?"

"Yes, sir."

"You wasn't at Goodman's farm on Friday, September 4 or Saturday, September 5?"

"No, sir, I was not."

"And if a man was at the farm on September 5, you wouldn't see him?"

"No, sir."

"You made that entry of his time from what someone else told you."

"Yes, sir."

"And if someone told you that Mr. Johnson was working at the farm, you would have noted him as having been there, would you?"

"Yes, sir."

"And you cannot testify to the work hours or the locations of the workers without testifying from the book, can you?"

"No, sir, I cannot."

Burritt says to the Court, "We renew our earlier objection."

Galbraith says, "I would also like to ask a question. By referring to the book for the purpose of refreshing your memory, Mr. Steele, can you testify as to the number of hours worked by Paul Johnson on the third, and fourth, and fifth of September?"

"By referring to the book I can."

"And by not refreshing your memory from the book."

"I could not. That is, I couldn't remember that he worked on the fourth and fifth without referring to the book, and even if I do look at the book, I can't recall any more than the book itself states."

Burritt says to the Court, "We renew our objection and insist upon it."

The Court says, "I think, under the circumstances, the admissibility of that evidence is doubtful."

Burritt says, "Certainly it is. The defense moves the Court to strike out the testimony of the witness, Mr. Steele, as he testified from the timesheets in the book and the testimony of the witness concerning the notation in the book as to where the man Mr. Johnson was on the fourth and fifth of September as incompetent, hearsay testimony."

The Court says, "I think I will let the evidence stand, for what it is worth, and give you an exception."

Burritt says, "My motion is, if the Court pleases, to strike it out as hearsay, that he cannot testify after refreshing his memory from the book. The witness says he don't know anything himself about the whereabouts of Johnson on the fourth and fifth of September."

The Court says, "All the testimony must be considered by the Court together on a motion of that kind and, consequently, I will let it stand and give you an exception."

Chapter 27
William Heikkila Recalled

Mr. Galbraith requests, "Your Honor, I also wish to call William Heikkila as a rebuttal witness."

Judge O'Brien says, "William Heikkila to the witness stand, please."

After being reminded that he is still under oath, Mr. Galbraith asks, "Referring to the testimony of Bill Lahnala, I ask if Bill Lahnala said to you when you were taking his statement in the sheriff's office, that when John came to his house on the evening of Saturday, September 5, that he, Bill, opened the door and John came in, and he was drunk?"

"Yes."

"Repeat, Mr. Heikkila, what Bill said as to John Lahnala's condition when he, Bill, opened the door."

"He said John rapped and that he was drunk and went to sleep."

Galbraith says, "John Lahnala testified that when you and Mr. Lucas and the other officer were questioning him, that you would not let him talk, but that you told him to only answer questions. I would ask you if that is true or not?"

"No sir, it is not true."

"What was your method of examining John Lahnala in the sheriff's office?"

"We asked him to give an account of himself, and he started to tell us where he was, and we questioned him also."

"Did you at any time prevent him from going ahead with his statement?"

"No, sir."

CROSS-EXAMINATION BY MR. BURRITT

Burritt asks, "And you left it to him to give you a full account of himself, didn't you, Mr. Heikkila?"

"And we questioned him also."

"Did you ask John Lahnala questions to get a detailed statement out of him, the same as we have done here at this trial?"

"Not so fully."

"And consequently, John Lahnala may have had some information or known some fact that you didn't get out of him."

"We thought we had everything that was to be gotten, but I guess we didn't get —"

Burritt interrupts, "You may have had more accurate and full information if you had asked the right questions or allowed him to speak more fully, is that so?"

"Yes."

"I have no more questions of this witness."

Galbraith says, "The People rest."

Judge O'Brien states, "It is getting late in the day. We will adjourn until 10 a.m. tomorrow morning.

Alex drives home after leaving court, eats dinner, and helps put the children down for the night. Hilda then asks, "Did anything exciting happen today in court?"

Alex replies, "Bill and Hannah both testified. Bill said he bought the pistol for his own protection during the mining strike. Hannah testified that she knows the pistol was in her drawer at home on September 5. She often saw it because she was always in that drawer.

"Judge O'Brien allowed testimony from a time book that William Burritt believes to be hearsay. The working hours of Paul Johnson, an employee of Goodman Lumber, are recorded in a book based on what somebody else said. That sounds like hearsay to me. The timekeeper didn't see the man working. He only recorded what he was told. But the judge allowed the testimony to stand!"

"Of more interest to me, John Lehto, the boarding house and bar owner in Hancock, testified that your father asked for lodging one night because someone said they'd kill him."

Hilda is wide-eyed and says, "Someone threatened my father's life? Along with other testimony on John's behalf, that should make some men on the jury think John is innocent."

"I agree." says Alex. "But right now, I'm ready for a good night's sleep. Good night."

Chapter 28
Bernard Goodman Recalled

When the court reconvenes the following morning, Mr. Burritt calls for Bernard J. Goodman to take the witness stand.

The Court reminds Mr. Goodman that he is still under oath.

William Burritt asks, "Now, Mr. Goodman, you heard Mr. Steele's testimony yesterday?"

"I did."

"Do you know where Mr. Paul Johnson worked on Saturday, the fifth of September, 1914?"

"Yes sir, at least after ten o'clock I do."

"Where?"

"He was whitewashing the mill."

"Who sent him there to work?"

"I did."

"Do you know whether he had been at the farm or not on September 4, Friday?"

"I couldn't swear to it, but I kind of think he was."

"Are you positive about his work on the fifth?"

"Yes sir, I sent Johnson and his partner to whitewash the mill."

"On Saturday, September 5, last?"

"Yes, sir."

"What was his partner's name?"

"I can't recall his last name, but his first name is Phil."

"Is the entry in the time book which purports to show that Mr. Johnson worked at the farm instead of working at the mill on September 5, 1914, correct as to fact or incorrect?"

"I can say it is incorrect as to fact."

"Does it sometimes happen that such mistakes are made in keeping the time book?"

"Yes, sir."

"Now, the time of the men is recorded by whom?"

"The time is turned in by the people after the work they are doing for the day, and Frank Steele asks what time is to be put down for the man. He then, of course, marks it down. Sometimes the bookkeeper marks it down."

Burritt says, "Thank you, Mr. Goodman. Mr. Galbraith, questions?"

"No questions," says Mr. Galbraith.

Chapter 29
Phillip Hoffman Testimony

After being sworn, Mr. Burritt asks, "What is your occupation, Mr. Hoffman?"

"I cook in the woods and do some loading work in Mr. Goodman's mill."

"Where were you working on Saturday, the fifth of September last?"

"We worked at the mill, whitewashed the mill."

"Was there any trouble with the whitewash machine?"

"Yes, she was leaking. We had too much air, and it broke open."

"And was Paul Johnson with you?"

"Yes, sir."

"And who told you to whitewash the mill?"

"Mr. Goodman."

"Now, how do you know it was September 5 when you worked whitewashing the mill?"

"I keep my own time. I got my own book, and I write it down; everything I buy, where I work, when I work in the mill or farm. I want to make sure we don't get mixed up."

Mr. Burritt says, "The defense rests, Your Honor."

The Court says, "Have you any more questions, Mr. Galbraith?"

Mr. Galbraith replies, "We do not, Your Honor."

BURRITT ADDRESSES THE COURT

Mr. Burritt rises to address the Court and says, "Your Honor, the defendant moves the Court to direct a verdict of not guilty in this case, on the grounds that the evidence is not sufficient to support a guilty verdict."

The Court says, "That motion is denied."

Chapter 30
Closing Arguments

BURRITT CLOSING ARGUMENT

At this point, the Court calls for Mr. Burritt to present his closing argument regarding the belief of the defense of the innocence of John Lahnala.

Burritt says, "Thank you, Your Honor.

"Gentlemen of the jury, to find a defendant guilty based on circumstantial evidence, the evidence must not only be consistent with the guilt of the defendant, it must also be inconsistent with all other possible scenarios. If there is another hypothesis which might explain what happened, it is your duty to find the defendant not guilty.

"In this case, you have heard several people state that they '*thought*' they saw the defendant at the candy store. You have also heard that they could not swear that it was him. On the other hand, the defense has produced witnesses who said they are positive they saw the defendant approximately one hundred miles away at the time of the murder. Gentlemen, he cannot be in two places at once, and we have presented witnesses who have testified under oath that the defendant was in southern Marquette County or Alger County."

Burritt continues and offers a lengthy summary of the holes in the prosecution's case.

GALBRAITH CLOSING ARGUMENT

At the conclusion of Burritt's argument, the Court requests Mr. Galbraith to offer the argument for the People and their belief that John Lahnala murdered his father. Galbraith's argument extends late into the day.

When Galbraith concludes, Judge O'Brien adjourns court for the day.

Chapter 31
Charge of the Court

The following morning, Judge O'Brien delivers the charge of the Court.

"Gentlemen of the jury, you have heard the evidence in this case. You have also heard the arguments of counsel. The case is a serious one.

"It now becomes the duty of the Court to charge you with the principles of the law and to apply them to the facts that you may find to be established by the evidence. It will then be your duty to render a fair, just, and impartial verdict.

"It is undisputed, that on the fifth day of September last, August Lahnala was murdered. John Lahnala, this defendant, who is a son of the deceased, is charged with his murder. The defendant has entered a plea of not guilty of the charge.

"Now, the People claim that they have established that the defendant and no other person murdered the deceased. Their entire case is based on circumstantial evidence. The law defines circumstantial evidence by saying that all evidence must point toward the guilt of the defendant, and in no other direction. There must be an unbroken chain, and if one link of that chain fails or is broken, the entire chain falls apart, and the jury must acquit the defendant. You will bear in mind that I am simply stating the claims made by the prosecution. I express no opinion as to whether or not any of the foregoing facts are established. That is a matter entirely for your determination and consideration.

"The prosecution has not introduced the testimony of any witness or witnesses who claim they saw the defendant take the train in the afternoon of September 4 at any place near Rumley for Houghton, nor any witness or witnesses who claim they saw the defendant on the train to Houghton, nor any witness or witnesses who claim they saw the defendant at the Houghton station taking the 10:55 p.m. train for the lower part of the Upper Peninsula, or saw him on that train on the night of September the fifth.

"The defendant has denied that he was in Houghton County on either Friday, September 4, or Saturday September 5. He denies that he had anything to do with the killing of his father. If, as the defendant claims, he was in Mr. Goodman's store between twelve and one o'clock on September the fifth, this makes it impossible that he came here and committed the murder, as claimed by the prosecution. Or if the defendant went to the house of Bill Lahnala on the night of September the fifth as Bill Lahnala and his wife, Hannah, testified he did, then he is not guilty and he should be acquitted.

"The defendant, gentlemen, is not obliged to prove his innocence. Everyone charged with crime is presumed to be innocent until the contrary is shown beyond a reasonable doubt. A reasonable doubt is a fair doubt based upon reason and common sense. It is such a doubt where you cannot say you have a moral certainty of the truth of the charge made against the defendant.

"It is the duty of every individual juror to consider the testimony and discuss it with his fellow jurors. If he has a reasonable doubt as to the guilt of the defendant, he should not convict him. And on the other hand, if any juror or jurors are convinced of the defendant's guilt beyond a reasonable doubt, such juror or jurors should not consent to a verdict of acquittal.

"A great deal of evidence in this case is in direct contradiction. It will, therefore, be necessary for you to weigh and carefully analyze the evidence of the different witnesses, to determine the facts from the evidence. You are the sole judges of the credibility of the witnesses and of the weight to be given to the testimony of each witness who has been sworn in this case.

"The first question that you will be called upon to determine is, was the defendant the person who shot and killed August Lahnala on the evening of the fifth of September 1914? The burden of proof is upon the prosecution to convince you beyond a reasonable doubt that it was the defendant and no other person who committed the homicide.

"Now, gentlemen, you recognize fully that you have a serious and important duty to perform. Weigh the evidence carefully. Consider all the facts and circumstances. If you are convinced beyond a reasonable doubt that this defendant is guilty, you will fearlessly bring in a verdict of 'Guilty of Murder in the First Degree.' On the other hand, if you are not convinced, you should equally as fearlessly bring in a verdict of 'Not Guilty.'"

Judge O'Brien completed his charge to the jury at 6:30 p.m. on Thursday, March 4, 1915.

Upon completion of the charge, Mr. Burritt has a request of the Court. "If the Court please, there are some exhibits here that the defense would like to have the jury take to their room. We would like to have the jury take with them the overalls, the pants, and the time book that have been introduced in evidence."

The Court says, "I think I will ask the jury to retire while this matter is discussed."

The jury here is escorted out of the courtroom.

Galbraith says, "Everything that has been offered in evidence, been offered and accepted, I think ought to go in if anything goes in."

Burritt agrees, "Yes, I am willing that all exhibits should all go to the jury."

The Court rules, "Under those circumstances, the jury will be permitted to have all of the exhibits, and the officers will now take all the exhibits to the jury room."

The following day, the local newspaper had an article about the trial status.

The Daily Mining Gazette

Friday, March 5, 1915

LAHNALA'S FATE HELD IN SUSPENSE BY JURY

Twelve Men Selected to Determine Guilt or Innocence of Boy Charged With Murder of His Father Deliberate All Night

The case of John Lahnala, on trial for the past three weeks on the charge of murdering his father at the family home on a farm at Oskar September 5, 1914, was given to the jury at 6:20 o'clock last evening by Judge O'Brien in the circuit court.

Prosecuting Attorney Galbraith completed his closing argument for the people shortly after 5 o'clock and Judge O'Brien decided that the jury should not be delayed in beginning its deliberations. He began his charge at once and completed it at 6:30.

At the conclusion of the charge Attorney Burritt, for the defense, asked that certain of the exhibits offered in evidence be sent into the jury room. Mr. Galbraith objected unless all the exhibits be sent in and the court finally ruled in favor of the latter idea.

Jury Locked Up for the Night

Judge O'Brien appeared in the court room at 9:30 o'clock and inquired of the jury if a verdict had been reached. Receiving a negative answer, he announced that court was adjourned 'til 9:15 this morning, which fixes the time for the reception of the verdict should it have been reached during the night.

Jury's Alternatives

In his charge to the jury last night Judge O'Brien left the twelve men with two alternatives. They must either find John Lahnala guilty of murder in the first degree or they must find him not guilty. The charge did not give the jury any latitude. There could be no question of guilt of a charge less than first-degree murder, such as second-degree murder or manslaughter.

The judge consumed considerable time in delivering his instructions to the jury and the charge is a voluminous document in itself. It could not be taken as inimical to the interests of the defendant.

For example, the court dwelt at length on the fact that no one saw Lahnala take a train for the Copper Country during the time he must have taken it to synchronize with the theory of the prosecution and no evidence is offered that anyone saw him on the train coming to Houghton.

The Court told the jury that they must be convinced beyond a reasonable doubt. The definition of such a doubt was provided by the Court.

Touching the circumstantial evidence, which is the basis of the state's case, the charge said the circumstances must exclude every other reasonable explanation than guilt to lead to conviction. It was explained that in a chain of circumstances offered as evidence of guilt every link must be proven to have a direct connection with the crime because "if a link is broken there is no chain."

Considering the statement made to the officers by John Lahnala at the time of his arrest, the court charged the jury to exercise great caution in weighing such a statement because at such a time the condition of the prisoner's mind might be such as to lead him into errors of memory.

The Closing Arguments

W. A. Burritt, senior counsel for the defense, occupied all of yesterday morning's session with his closing argument. Mr. Burritt is a man of tremendous force as a pleader, and he made a powerful argument. He analyzed the evidence of all the witnesses and argued for fatal weaknesses in various links in the prosecution's chain of circumstances, as well as offering as a complete alibi the testimony of B. J. Goodman and Paul Johnson, that they had seen Lahnala at Little Lake on the day of the murder.

Prosecuting Attorney Galbraith occupied the entire afternoon session with his closing argument for the prosecution. He offered as a complete chain of evidence all the circumstances testified by the state's witnesses.

Mr. Galbraith dwelt at length on the alleged motive for the murder: Lahnala's father's refusal to buy John suitable clothing. He said that this condition rankled in the boy's heart 'til it gave birth to a murderous resolve and, from then on, he followed out the chain of circumstances that appeared to him to prove that the boy had plotted patricide.

Chapter 32
The Verdict

When the court reconvenes on March 6, people line the walls to hear what they expect will be a verdict of not guilty. There are no vacant seats in the courtroom. There is an atmosphere of hushed anticipation.

Judge O'Brien starts the proceedings by stating to those in the courtroom, "I want to remind all of you that this is a court of law and order. I will not tolerate any outburst of emotion which might disrupt the orderly due process of the law!"

The prosecution sits with tightened lips when Judge O'Brien asks, "Gentlemen of the jury, have you reached a verdict?"

The jury foreman replies, "We have, Your Honor."

Alex and John look at each other, and Alex is struck by John's appearance. He looks calm and apparently confident of a not guilty verdict.

The Court asks, "And what is your finding?"

The jury foreman replied, "We the jury, find the defendant guilty of first-degree murder."

The courtroom erupts with emotional shouts of "What!" and "How in the world could you?" and some much stronger statements. Judge O'Brien pounds his gavel and shouts "Order! Order in the court!" which does not soothe those in attendance. Judge O'Brien adjourns the court for thirty minutes to clear the room and to let emotions subside.

When court reconvenes, many of the reporters are missing, presumably gone to submit their stories to their editors. Other people have lost interest and simply wandered away. Mr. Galbraith, satisfied with the verdict, says, "At this time, Your Honor, on behalf of the People, I move that the Court sentence the defendant based on the verdict as returned by the jury."

Judge O'Brien replies, "The Court will defer passing sentence until Monday morning, at which time sentence will be passed at the opening of court."

Alex thinks, *The judge was as surprised as many in the courtroom. He was anticipating a verdict of not guilty and hadn't prepared for a guilty verdict.*

The Daily Mining Gazette

Sunday, March 7, 1915

JOHN LAHNALA IS GUILTY OF HIS FATHER'S DEATH

Celebrated Murder Trial Comes to End with Verdict of the Jury of Guilty of Murder in the First Degree
Lahnala Keeps His Nerve

John Lahnala was found guilty yesterday morning by the jury in the circuit court of the murder of his father, August Lahnala, at Oskar on the night of September 5, 1914. The case went to the jury at 6:30 Friday evening and the verdict was given at 10:15 yesterday morning. Those in the crowded courtroom were aghast at the verdict and Judge O'Brien took a thirty-minute adjournment to allow sentiments to cool.

Burritt & Burritt, attorneys for the defense, will take the case to the Supreme Court and W. A. Burritt, senior counsel, has expressed his firm conviction that the highest tribunal in the state will free the youth on the record of the trial.

The youthful defendant, who through the trial has maintained a wonderfully impassive demeanor, did not lose his nerve when his fate was pronounced by the jury. He heard the verdict without a tremor or a change of expression and he walked from the court room as unconcerned as the officer who accompanied him.

The duration of the trial, three weeks, and the fact that the case turned on evidence that was circumstantial, wholly aroused great public interest in the case. There naturally was a great difference of opinion and some people are convinced that Lahnala established a complete alibi. The jury was not convinced of the purity of the alibi, however.

The attorneys for the defense moved for a stay of sentence but Judge O'Brien refused to grant it and announced he will sentence tomorrow morning. As the Court's charge to the jury said, the verdict if "guilty," must be for murder in the first degree. The court has no alternative but to impose a life sentence, the second time Judge O'Brien has had to impose this sentence since his elevation to the bench.

Ballots of the Jury

The verdict was announced to the court by Alex A. Barbeau of Lake Linden, foreman of the jury. Following the discharge of the jury a member gave out the fact that five ballots only had been taken. The first three stood eight for conviction and four for acquittal. The fourth ballot found only two holding out for acquittal and the fifth was unanimous.

In the next issue, the following article appeared in the local newspaper.

The Daily Mining Gazette

Tuesday, March 9, 1915

JOHN LAHNALA HEARS HIS FATE WITHOUT EMOTION

Youthful Convicted Patricide is Unshaken as Judge O'Brien Pronounces Life Sentence Immense Crowd Hears Fate Pronounced

John Lahnala, convicted on Saturday of the crime of murdering his father at Oskar September 5, 1914, was yesterday sentenced to serve the remainder of his life at Marquette Prison by Judge O'Brien in the circuit court.

The youthful, convicted murderer heard his fate without a tremor, maintaining the cold indifference that has characterized his demeanor throughout the trial. The youth was brought to the bar immediately on the opening of court and the court put forth the usual question: "Have you anything to say why sentence should not be pronounced against you?"

"I am not guilty in this case." said Lahnala and from then on he heard the judge's comments and sentence without visible emotion.

"The jury has settled that," said the judge in response to Lahnala's assertion. "It is unfortunate that a young man as bright as you are should have allowed a settled hatred against his father to grow until it impelled him to murder. The jury has said that you are guilty of this murder."

"You have had a fair trial. Your witnesses were subpoenaed by the state at its expense. You had the ablest counsel who conducted your defense with zeal and devotion. The jury was impartial. They fully considered the testimony, and no man can criticize their verdict."

"As a Court, I have no opinion to offer and no authority to judge questions of fact submitted in your case. But in your case, I have no criticism of the verdict. Therefore, while it is a painful duty, it is nonetheless a duty that must be performed. The statute leaves the Court no alternative and the sentence of the Court is that you be sent to the branch state prison for the Upper Peninsula at Marquette for the term of your life."

Lahnala sat down the instant the court uttered the last quoted sentence and began a whispered conversation with his attorney, B. H. T. Burritt. He was at once removed by the sheriff and taken to his cell to await transportation to Marquette.

Undersheriff Heikkila took Lahnala to Marquette yesterday afternoon. The boy continued to display his iron nerve and he even smiled at acquaintances in the crowd of 200 or more who gathered at the station platform to feast their eyes on a murderer. He nonchalantly rolled a cigarette while waiting for the train and boarded it with the officer as unconcerned as though he was embarking for a pleasure tour.

Echo of Murder Case

St. Clair Wilson, deputy State of Michigan Game Warden for Houghton County on Saturday night served on Bill Lahnala, brother of John, a warrant issued in Alger County, charging Bill Lahnala with a violation of the game laws. This follows testimony given both by John and Bill in the murder trial. They testified that on Sunday, September 6 they went hunting at Rumley, Alger County, Bill's home, and that they killed a deer. This happened about two months before the opening of legal deer season. A warrant also was issued for John Lahnala but his conviction of the murder and his sentence to Marquette prison makes it inoperative.

Chapter 33
St. Cyr Phone Call

On March 18, 1915, William Burritt receives a call from Albert St. Cyr, who is a train conductor for the Munising, Marquette & Southeastern Railroad Company. St. Cyr says he can vouch for John Lahnala being near Rumley the afternoon of September 5, 1914.

On March 22, 1915, William Burritt takes the train from Houghton to Marquette. He meets with Albert St. Cyr at the Little Lake train depot.

Burritt says, "Mr. St. Cyr, I understand you're a conductor on the train that runs between Marquette and Rumley."

St. Cyr replies, "That's correct."

Burritt asks, "I was told that you recall John Lahnala riding that train on September 5, last."

"That's correct," St. Cyr says.

"Why do you remember that specific date?" Burritt asked.

St. Cyr says, "Well, it's kind of unusual. I recall a young man boarded the train at Little Lake and wanted to go to Rumley. But he didn't have a ticket. So, I collected the cash fare from him and reprimanded him for not having a ticket. He seemed unusually sensitive when I spoke with him, and I developed a vivid mental picture of his face and dress. Also, the fare I collected from him was the only cash fare I received that trip. I also told him he'd have to change trains at Lawson Junction."

Burritt says, "I see. Please go on."

"A couple of days later, on September 8, 1914, I heard of the murder of August Lahnala. A sheriff's deputy from the Copper Country was on the train looking for a young Finn, John Lahnala, who he described to me and who was accused of the crime. I immediately thought of the young man who rode with me the evening of September 5, but I didn't say anything because I didn't think it possible that he rode on the train with me. I thought that would be quite a coincidence.

"After I heard that Lahnala was convicted, I heard some of the details of the case and that he testified that he boarded a train here for Rumley and was reprimanded by the conductor. That got me to thinking. I went to the company's office in Marquette and looked at my train checks for September 5 and found, as I expected, that there was only one cash fare slip from Little Lake to Lawson.

"Eight days ago, I went to the Marquette Branch Prison for the express purpose of identifying the man I referred to. There were over three hundred prisoners in the yard, but I had no difficulty identifying John Lahnala, and I know positively that he is the man who rode on the train on September 5, 1914."

Burritt asks, "Are you now willing to testify as you have just told me?"

St. Cyr replies, "I will. I must try to clear my conscience."

Burritt says, "Thank you, we appreciate that! You'll hear from me again." Burritt then excuses himself so he could return to Houghton.

Ten days later Alex and Hilda are in Hancock, shopping for kitchen supplies. Alex suggests they drop in at the Burritt law firm to see if the attorneys have an update on their efforts to secure a new trial. They are pleased to learn the news about St. Cyr and his willingness to testify.

Alex looks at William and says, "We haven't seen John for almost a month, and I think it would lift his spirits if we visited him at the Marquette prison. If we can make the arrangements, do you mind if we mention the St. Cyr development to John?"

William looks at Barney and says, "Not at all! It would please him, I'm sure."

Barney recommends, "The Windsor Hotel is a great place if you plan to spend the night. I had good service when I stayed there last October."

Hilda asks Barney, "Do you know if it's possible to take the train to Marquette, spend a nice evening there, visit John the next day, and get home the same day?"

Barney replies, "It will be a late night getting there, so I suggest you make it a two-night trip. You'll have a better opportunity to visit with John and still get home the second day."

Alex thinks out loud, "I'm sure we can get help with our chores and children if we explain that we want to visit John. And I want to let John know that he hasn't been forgotten. Let's see if we can make this happen." Three days later, they are on the train to Marquette.

Barney Burritt has suggested that Alex and Hilda get a room at the Windsor Hotel. When they get to Marquette, a car and driver from the hotel are waiting for them at the train station, compliments of Barney. They settle in for a short night and talk about their visit with John.

After they wake in the morning, Alex and Hilda enjoy a leisurely breakfast before taking a taxi to the prison less than three miles away. Alex has heard that the architecture of the prison is impressive, and he is not disappointed. The buildings are constructed of beautiful brown sandstone, but the gardens, which are maintained by the prisoners, are the most impressive.

Hilda jokingly makes a comment about this place not looking like a bad place to live. Alex frowns at her and she apologizes.

After entering the main gate and announcing why they are there, they are escorted to the cell block where John is housed. A short time later, John joins them, and Hilda sheds some tears when she sees her brother in prison garb. They only have thirty minutes for discussion, so Alex tells John that Burritt & Burritt are busy preparing a filing for a new trial.

Alex says, "Albert St. Cyr is a train conductor who heard about your trial. He collected the fare from you on the night of your father's murder. We feel that there's an excellent chance that his testimony will be sufficient to get a new trial!"

"That's great news!" replies John.

Alex adds, "And, of course, Barney and William feel that the Court erred many times in its decisions regarding testimony of several witnesses. That may be the most important factor in deciding whether a new trial is granted.

"But the Burritt team and I have also agreed to a slightly different approach if we can get a new trial. We want to concentrate more on testimony of witnesses such as St. Cyr, who can vouch for you being in the Rumley area."

Hilda interjected, "The legal fight certainly continues, John. And I want to let you know that your family continues to pray for your release. All I hear when I'm out and about is disbelief that the jury found you guilty. Nobody can understand that!"

The remainder of their time together is spent talking about recent events in their family. All too soon their time is over, and John gives Alex and Hilda warm hugs before they are escorted out.

Two days later, the following article appears in *The Daily Mining Gazette.*

The Daily Mining Gazette

Thursday, April 8, 1915

MOVE FOR A NEW TRIAL

Burritt & Burritt Have New Evidence in the Lahnala Case

Attorney B. H. T. Burritt of the firm of Burritt & Burritt, Hancock, counsel for the defense in the John Lahnala murder case, announced yesterday the intention of the firm to move for a new trial on the grounds of new and important evidence.

Mr. Burritt says that Conductor St. Cyr of the Marquette and Southeastern railroad in Marquette County swears that John Lahnala rode on his train through Alger County on the night he was reported to be in Oskar, Houghton County, murdering his father.

On April 30, 1915, Burritt & Burritt filed a motion with the Houghton County Circuit Court for a new trial. They request that the verdict of the jury and the judgment of the Court be vacated and set aside and a new trial be granted. The firm lists the items of which they believed the Court erred. They also added a new item: newly discovered evidence which was the affidavit of Albert St. Cyr, in which he said John Lahnala was on his train the evening of September 5, 1914.

On May 14, 1915, the Circuit Court filed its legal opinion denying the motion for a new trial. In its denial, the Court explains each of the items in which the defendant feels that the Court erred. Regarding the new item, the Court believes that the new testimony would only duplicate testimony that was already given. Would St. Cyr's testimony result in a different verdict in the trial? The Court doesn't believe it would. In its filing, the Court also said, "The evidence of the witnesses who identified John Lahnala as being in Houghton County was clear and positive."

The following day, the paper reported the following:

The Daily Mining Gazette

Saturday, May 15, 1915

LAHNALA MOTION DENIED

At a late hour yesterday afternoon Judge O'Brien denied the motion for a new trial for John Lahnala, convicted this year of murdering his father and now serving a life sentence in Marquette State Prison.

Attorneys Burritt & Burritt intimated when the motion was argued last Monday that if it were denied they would go to the Michigan Supreme Court with it.

Chapter 34
Supreme Court

The Burritt & Burritt law firm threatened to go to the Michigan Supreme Court if the Circuit Court denied its motion for a new trial. Now the firm has to decide whether to proceed with the threatened action or lick its wounds and move on with other business. If it decides to proceed, the cost of doing so must be considered. "Cost" in this case would mean the financial cost of arguing a case in front of Michigan's highest court, as well as the professional cost if the Supreme Court decided that the case brought by Burritt & Burritt didn't have any legal merit.

"I don't know, Dad," says Barney Burritt. "We can't expect the Lahnala family to pay for this appeal. They simply cannot afford it."

William Burritt responds, "That's true enough. But think of the professional benefit we'd get if we did go ahead with this. Not many legal firms get the chance to argue a case at the Michigan Supreme Court. I've been in this business a long time and have never had this opportunity. This is likely my only chance. You may never get the chance again, Barney. If we proceed, we'll be in an elite group of legal firms. If we win, the reputation of Burritt & Burritt will certainly be enhanced. It's a big decision. Let's sleep on this and discuss it further tomorrow."

William Burritt is sixty-two years old, is financially set, and has a solid professional reputation. But he also has an ego. The thought of bringing a case before the Michigan Supreme Court appeals strongly to him. He has practiced law for thirty-one years, and this could be a huge feather in his cap. He also strongly feels that the Circuit Court has made significant errors in the Lahnala case, and he feels that the Supreme Court will agree. But the bottom line is his strong feeling that John Lahnala is innocent. He must do what he can to prove him innocent.

Barney understands, at least partially, his father's feelings. Barney also respects his father's legal acumen and reputation. But arguing a case to the Michigan Supreme Court? He never thought that his father would go that far.

The following morning, Barney and his father meet again. William starts the discussion by asking, "In your gut, do you think John murdered his father?"

"I don't see how he could have," replies Barney.

William agrees. "I don't either. And that's why we must get a new trial for him. I believe that the Circuit Court ruled incorrectly several times, and its actions may have helped us build a solid case in appeal. Morally, we have no option but to proceed. Forget the financial cost! If we must, we'll eat the cost ourselves. Do you agree?"

Barney is surprised at his father's conviction. He has never seen his father express himself so forcefully. But he has to agree. "Yes!"

William says, "Thank you, son! Now we must get to work. We'll review the transcript of the trial and see how many exceptions were granted by Judge O'Brien. Then we must review the law in those cases where the Court ruled against us to determine our strongest legal points. These will be the issues we'll take to the Supreme Court."

William and Barney phone Alex and Hilda and ask them to come to their office to discuss what they plan to do. Alex says, "We plan to be in Hancock the day after tomorrow to buy supplies. Can we meet then?"

William replies, "That will be fine."

On May 18, 1915, Alex and Hilda go to the Burritt & Burritt offices. After they are all seated, William explains the basics of their plan to Alex and Hilda.

Alex takes Hilda's hand and says to William and Barney, "We're convinced that John could not have killed August. But we cannot afford to proceed. Unless something dramatic happens, there is little we can do to help financially."

William gives Barney a glance and says, "Barney and I have discussed the matter. As we said when you first hired us, we're convinced that John did not do this. And it's time to put our money where our mouth is, so to speak. If you are willing to proceed, we will continue the fight for John's freedom without further financial support from you."

Hilda looks at Alex and starts to cry. Alex hugs her and also gets teary-eyed.

"I never expected you to go this far!" Hilda exclaims through her tears. "We cannot expect you to do this."

Barney replies, "But we have decided that we will. Father and I plan to review the trial testimony and be more aggressive in our investigation in the Rumley area. Mr. St. Cyr has further convinced us of John's truthfulness. Also, the testimony of those who said they saw John at Gekas' Candy Kitchen is doubtful at best.

We feel that the Supreme Court will rule in our favor once they see the evidence. We plan to get started on our appeal to the Supreme Court tomorrow."

Having never appealed a case to the Michigan Supreme Court, William and Barney don't know how much time it would take to prepare. Somehow, they must make time to handle their other cases as well as review all of the legal points and the trial transcript from John's first trial.

Finally, on January 17, 1916, their arguments and the records from the first trial are sent to the Supreme Court. They are advised that a Supreme Court decision would likely not occur for several months.

In the August 16, 1916 *Daily Mining Gazette* in Houghton, Michigan, a small article appears.

The Daily Mining Gazette

Wednesday, August 16, 1916

Lahnala Counsel Passes

After working diligently to secure a new trial for John Lahnala, on August 15, 1916 William A. Burritt, primary counsel for John Lahnala, passed away at the age of 63 at his home in Hancock. The cause of death was diabetes mellitus, more commonly known as sugar diabetes. He suffered the effects of this disease for 21 years. It caused problems with Mr. Burritt's feet which eventually led to gangrene and his death. Mr. Burritt's son, Barney H. T. Burritt, has been William Burritt's legal partner since he was admitted to the bar in 1904. He continues to practice at his office in Hancock.

Alex and Hilda cannot believe it. They are aware that William's health has been declining, and they hadn't seen or talked to him for several weeks. But they never expected his death to be imminent. They call the Marquette Branch Prison to share the news with John. As they talk, they can hear John fighting back tears. John asks how this will affect plans for a second trial, and Alex explains that he is sure Barney will go ahead with their plans.

Alex calls Barney and expresses the condolences of the entire family. Barney appreciates the sentiments and explains that this has been a difficult time for his family. He apologizes and lets Alex know that his father wished to be buried in North Lansing, Michigan. He is currently making funeral arrangements. Alex apologizes for the interruption and asks Barney to call him when he's back in the area. Barney says he certainly will.

Nine days later, Barney calls to set up a dinner with Alex and Hilda. When they get together, Hilda says she appreciated the opportunity to get to know William. "I'm so sorry for your loss, Barney. He was an influential man, and I respected him and the work he did on behalf of our family."

Barney replies, "Thank you. I know he fully believed in John's innocence and wanted another chance to prove it. Unfortunately, he won't get that chance. But I plan to carry that torch and see it through!"

Barney then provides an update on their plea to the Michigan Supreme Court by saying he hasn't heard much, but the Court should be reviewing their case soon.

Six weeks later, on October 3, 1916, Barney Burritt gets word of the biggest victory of the legal team of Burritt & Burritt:

The Supreme Court of the State of Michigan

In session at the Supreme Court Room, in the Capitol, in the City of Lansing, on the third day of October in the year of our Lord one thousand nine hundred and sixteen,

Present the Honorable
John W. Stone, Chief Justice

Associate Justices

Franz C. Kuhn
John E. Bird
Joseph H. Steere
Russell C. Ostrander
Joseph B. Moore
Flavius L. Brooke
Rollin H. Person

THE PEOPLE OF THE STATE OF MICHIGAN, Plaintiff
vs.
John Lahnala, Defendant.

The record and proceedings in this cause having been removed to this court by Writ of Error, issued to the Circuit Court for the County of Houghton, and the same, and the matters in error assigned, have been seen and inspected and duly considered by the Court, and it appearing to the Court that in said record and proceedings, and in the giving of judgment in said Circuit Court there is manifest error. Therefore, it is ordered and adjudged by the Court that the judgment of said Circuit Court for the County of Houghton be and the same is hereby reversed and vacated, the verdict set aside and a new trial granted. The Defendant will be delivered into the custody of the Sheriff of Houghton County, to be dealt with according to law.

In typical legalese fashion, it took thirteen pages, but the result was a new trial.

Barney's elation is tempered by the fact that his father cannot be with him to celebrate. Barney is sure that, somehow, his father knows.

Upon hearing the news, Barney calls Alex and exclaims, "We have a new trial!"

"Excellent! Fantastic job, Burritt & Burritt!" replies Alex. "After talking so much to your father and you, I had a strong feeling the Supreme Court would agree to your plea. Now you have some legal work to get done. Please let me know when and how I can help."

Barney agrees, "True. Much work! You helped a lot on our defense of John in the first trial, Alex. I'm asking for more of your help on the second trial because my father is not here to bounce ideas off. I'll call you soon to see when you're available."

The next day, *The Daily Mining Gazette* of Houghton reports:

The Daily Mining Gazette

Wednesday, October 4, 1916

Supreme Court of Michigan Orders New Trial

Lahnala Trial in January
Man Charged with Murder of Father
Won't Be Tried Next Term

B. H. T. Burritt, attorney for John Lahnala who was sentenced to serve a life term in the Marquette prison for the murder of his father at Oskar several months ago, has been granted a new trial by the Michigan Supreme Court. The Supreme Court determined that there was "manifest error" during his circuit court trial meaning there was indisputable error of judgment and complete disregard of the facts of the case and the applicable rule of law. Mr. Burritt's client will not be tried at the November term of the Houghton County circuit court. It is likely the trial will be included in the January term.

Attorney Barney Burritt says Lahnala will be returned to Houghton County from the Marquette prison at an early date. Owing to the amount of work that will be necessary to prepare the case for trial, the defendant's counsel does not believe it will be possible to arrange to have the new case ready for next month.

Chapter 35
New Trial Preparations

As promised, Barney calls Alex and asks when he's available so they can put their heads together to plan the defense.

"Tuesday works for me," says Alex. "And I have a couple of ideas."

"Great, Tuesday it is. I thought you'd have some ideas. Dinner at the Douglas House is on me," Barney volunteers. "I'm hoping Hilda won't be upset, but I'd like this meeting to be just the two of us. I want to make this a working meeting to get some good ideas on the table."

"I'm sure that will be fine with Hilda," replies Alex. "Her main interest is a not guilty verdict for John. I'll explain things to her."

At 6:00 p.m. on October 10, 1916 Alex meets with Barney in the same Douglas House conference room where they first met just over two years ago.

"Things are certainly different now than the first time we met here," says Barney.

"That's for sure. I wish your father were here to add his wisdom," replies Alex.

"Yes. I certainly miss him. He took me from being a little boy to the Michigan Supreme Court. Who else can say that?" Barney adds warmly.

"He was a good man, and I thank you for allowing Hilda and me to get to know him." adds Alex.

"It was my pleasure. Should we get started with our prep work for the second trial?" asks Barney.

"Yes." Alex replies.

Barney says, "You said you had a couple of ideas about the new trial. Want to share them?"

Alex says, "Sure. After Albert St. Cyr came forward and said after the first trial that he's positive he saw John, I started to think that it might make sense to concentrate more on getting witnesses from the Rumley area to prove that John was there, rather than disproving he was in the Houghton area. In the last trial, there was much finger-pointing between local friends and calling them liars. Perhaps not using that specific word.

"There is an old saw which goes, 'You can catch more flies with honey than with vinegar.' The finger-pointing didn't sit well with me. As I watched the reaction of the jurors, I don't think it sat well with some members of the jury either. Proving where John *was* when his father was killed might be more well received by a jury."

Barney thinks Alex is on to something and replies, "My father always thought he had to address and disprove the points the prosecution made. I have to agree with my father; that's important especially if we have clear evidence. But I understand what you're saying. I will still need to disprove some supposed 'facts,' but maybe I shouldn't carry my arguments to the extreme that my father did."

Alex is pleased with Barney's response and continues, "I've also been thinking about a saying I've heard for years: 'Blood is thicker than water.' I've wondered if the jury thought that "blood" testimony — that is, testimony which is given by close relatives — might be biased to favor John. If the jury thought it's biased, it might help explain the first verdict."

Barney wonders about that concept. After a minute or two, he says, "I also have a couple of ideas. Alex, you mentioned in the first trial that you didn't like many of my father's exceptions to the Court's rulings. Of course, my father used that technique to try to secure a new trial if the verdict didn't go our way. You do realize that these very exceptions are a primary reason why the Michigan Supreme Court ruled to give John a new trial, don't you?"

Alex says, "Yes, I understand that. But at the same time, I saw the jury's reaction to some of the exceptions, and several jurors shook their heads, or pursed their lips, or adjusted their positions in their chairs when they heard your father say "Exception." It appeared to me that as the trial wore on, they increasingly disliked the word."

"That's interesting," replies Barney. "As I think about it, the Supreme Court has had their say in John's case by granting John a new trial. If there are issues with the way the second trial is handled and John is found guilty again, I doubt very much if the Supreme Court would grant another appeal. So, there is no reason for me to take as many exceptions to the rulings of the Circuit Court. That would be pointless. I'll be very careful before taking that action in the second trial!"

Barney continues, "Also, that kind of sets the stage for how I'd like to conduct our defense in the new trial. I don't want to get into the legal technicalities if we have a face-off with the prosecution. I also don't want the picture we present to the jury to be forgotten or distorted by too many confusing objections."

After two hours of bouncing ideas off each other, Alex feels that Barney will be less contradictory than his father was, which might be better seen by the judge and jury. They don't imagine that the prosecution's case can be much different than it was in the first trial.

They review the list of witnesses from the first trial and agree that Barney should be able to shoot holes in most of the testimony of prosecution witnesses based on what came up in the first trial. The defense part of the trial will rely mainly on testimony from witnesses who Barney, Alex, and others have interviewed and who will provide alibis for John being in the Rumley area. That is the basis of the case for the defense: shoot holes in the prosecution's evidence and rely on defense witnesses who saw John in the Rumley area.

Alex feels that this meeting with Barney was important in defining how this trial will be conducted and in his relationship with Barney. Barney seems appreciative of Alex's ideas as he bids Alex a safe journey home when the meeting ends. As Alex drives home, he becomes more optimistic and is anxious to tell his wife about their discussion. After hearing what Alex says, Hilda is enthusiastic about the new trial also.

Chapter 36
Trial Commences

The second murder trial for John Lahnala commenced on Wednesday, Feb. 21, 1917. As in the first trial, the Honorable Patrick H. O'Brien is the Circuit Court Judge. The people are represented by William Merrill, prosecuting attorney. Attorney B. H. T. Burritt, "Barney", represents John Lahnala. Twenty-three potential jurors are interviewed by the conclusion of voir dire, the jury selection process. Twelve jurors and three alternates are selected by the time Court adjourns on February 22, 1917.

The Daily Mining Gazette

Thursday, February 22, 1917

JOHN LAHNALA IS AGAIN ON TRIAL CHARGED WITH THE MURDER OF HIS FATHER

Oskar Youth Faces Jury for the Second Time
Prospect That the Trial Will Occupy the Court for Succeeding Two Weeks

John Lahnala of Oskar was yesterday placed on trial for the second time on a charge of having murdered his father. He served more than a year in Marquette on conviction of the same charge, was granted a new trial, and has been awaiting the call to court for several months in the Houghton County jail.

In the more than two years that have elapsed since his first arrest, Lahnala has developed somewhat. He was boyish in appearance at the first trial but now seems to have attained manhood. He is a good-looking young fellow, a decided blonde and his light complexion is heightened by the proverbial prison pallor. He is taking the proceedings calmly.

August Lahnala, father of the defendant, was called to the door of his farm home at Oskar, the night of September 5, 1915 and shot dead. No one saw the shooting.

John, who had been living with a brother in Alger County, was arrested, tried for the murder of his father, and convicted on circumstantial evidence. Prosecuting Attorney Merrill stated to the jury yesterday morning that the case for the people still relies on circumstantial evidence to convict.

Stiff Legal Fight Promised

Lahnala was defended in the first trial by the late W. A. Burritt of Hancock. B. H. T. Burritt, son of the deceased attorney, is conducting this trial. He made it evident yesterday morning at the start that he is going to fight every step of the way through the trial.

On Friday, February 23,1917, the trial proper begins as the Court asks, "Mr. Merrill, are you ready with your opening statement?"

Merrill replies, "I am, Your Honor."

The Court says, "Please proceed."

"Of course, Your Honor."

"Gentlemen of the jury, September 5, 1914, was a Saturday, and August Lahnala was pressing hay. After the work was done, Mr. Lahnala and the others working with him had dinner at the Lahnala home in Oskar. When they finished their meal, the workers separated; some went home, those who lived with August relaxed at the Lahnala home. By 7 p.m., most of the Lahnala family were preparing to turn in for the night. August wanted to get some supplies, so he went to the nearby store in Oskar.

"Arriving home about an hour later, August entered the kitchen and then answered a knock at the door. He was met with three shots from a pistol. One of them took his life. The occupants of the house tried to call the sheriff, but the phone was dead. They were afraid to go outside to get help for fear they might meet the same fate.

"The People will show that the defendant, John Lahnala, was residing in Alger County at the time of the shooting. We will also show that there was bad blood between the defendant and his father, August, for a significant amount of time prior to the murder.

"Witnesses for the People will state that they saw the defendant in a Houghton store the night before the murder. Other witnesses will state that the defendant had access to a pistol of the same caliber as that which caused the death of the victim, August Lahnala.

"You will hear statements that say the defendant was in southern Marquette County or Alger County on the morning of September 6, 1914. The People will show that it is possible to leave Houghton on the train and be in that area early the next morning.

"In summary, the case of the People will establish the facts which show that the defendant had the motive, the means, and the opportunity, which are the three main general elements to commit a crime. Other elements will be revealed as the case is developed. I simply ask that you keep an open mind regarding the presumption of innocence.

"Thank you."

The Court says, "Thank you, Mr. Merrill. Mr. Burritt, your opening statement, please."

As Barney Burritt rises from his seat to present his opening statement, he sips some water to soothe his dry mouth. He approaches the jury, and his mind whirls. *This is your big chance, Barney! Keep cool, stick to what you've learned. You know John is innocent. Show these men what you know to be true.* He coughs to clear his throat and, with a courteous tone of voice, confidently starts his defense.

"Gentlemen of the jury, this young man is charged with murdering his father. The People have provided circumstantial evidence in the hope that this evidence will lead you to conclude that he committed this crime. Every syllable of their evidence is circumstantial.

"The Court has defined circumstantial evidence by saying it is inferred. That is to say, it is indirect. There are no witnesses to any of it. The Court has also said that all circumstantial evidence must point toward the guilt of the defendant, and in no other direction. There must be an unbroken chain, and if one link of that chain is broken, the entire chain falls apart, and the jury must acquit the defendant.

"If you are not convinced of the validity of any prosecution argument or assumption, if you have a reasonable doubt, the prosecution's case falls apart because that theory has not been firmly established in your mind.

"The law of the State of Michigan is that this boy is presumed to be innocent of this crime. Every man on this jury must say he is innocent until the facts presented here convince every man on this jury that he is guilty to a moral certainty.

"The theory of the prosecution is that John Lahnala was in the Copper Country on September 4, 1914. But there isn't one syllable of hard evidence which shows that he was in this area. The Defense will show that the testimony of Prosecution witnesses is suspect.

"The Defense will present testimony of several witnesses who will tell you that this boy was in the southern part of the Upper Peninsula near Rumley after noon on Friday, September 4, the whole day of Saturday, September 5, and the morning of Sunday, September 6. This testimony will clearly show that the case of the Prosecution has not been established.

"It may be helpful, gentlemen, to paint a word picture. The Prosecution will provide information which will paint a big picture for you. That picture might consist of statements showing that the defendant and his father didn't get along, for example. From a distance, this may appear to be accurate. However, not everything can be seen from far away. The details would not be visible, and you wouldn't see the true picture. The Defense will fill in those details so you will see the true picture.

"It really is that simple. The testimony of the Defense witnesses will make you doubt if the defendant was on the train to Houghton on September 4, or of being in the Houghton area the evening of September 4, or when the murder was committed the evening of September 5, or of being on the train back to Rumley that evening. If you have any doubts, the law says you must find the defendant not guilty of this crime.

"In addition, we will introduce evidence that there was more than one person who was an enemy of August Lahnala, and that August lived in fear of them. There will also be evidence introduced to show that there are other theories that were worthy of investigation other than the theory that was followed by the officers in this case. But these other theories received little or no attention.

"The case of the Defense will show that the case of the Prosecution has holes large enough to ride a horse through. We will prove through testimony that John Lahnala was not in the Houghton area when this crime was committed. It really is that simple, gentlemen.

"Thank you."

The next day, the following article appeared in *The Daily Mining Gazette.*

The Daily Mining Gazette

Saturday, February 24, 1917

LAHNALA CASE BEGUN

Jury Selection to Try John Lahnala on Charge of Murdering His Father is Completed - Trial is in Progress

Case Attracts Attention

The John Lahnala case is attracting considerable attention and at both sessions yesterday the court room was crowded. An interesting group of spectators was made up of the senior class of the Adams Township high school at Painesdale, 23 bright boys and girls. The court officers facilitated their study of the case by giving them front seats and furnishing each with a copy of the court calendar. They were taking industrious notes throughout the session.

Mr. William Merrill, the attorney for the people, made an opening statement to the jury. In a general way the facts that the prosecution will attempt to prove are well known. August Lahnala, father of the defendant, was shot at the door of his home the night of September 5, 1914. The son, John, had left home some time before and had been living with a brother in Alger County. The prosecution alleges that he left that county and came to Houghton County to kill his father, returning immediately to Alger County. The prosecution's proofs of this theory will be developed through the testimony.

Mr. Merrill admits that the people rely wholly on circumstantial evidence, there being no eyewitnesses to the shooting.

Mr. Barney Burritt is the attorney defending John Lahnala, who has already served two years of a life sentence for this charge. Burritt's opening statement reiterated that he intends to rely on several alibis to defend John, putting forth testimony to prove that he was in southern Marquette County or Alger County at the time his father was shot and that therefore he could not have done the shooting.

Chapter 37
Prosecution Witness Testimonies

Mr. Merrill calls Herbert Lahnala as the first witness for the People. Herbert takes the witness stand, and Merrill says, "Please state your name."

"Herbert Lahnala."

"You live with your mother?"

"Yes."

"What was your father doing the night he was killed?"

"We ate dinner, and then he went to Hermanson's store."

"Did you hear when he came home?"

"Yes."

"Where were you when he came home?"

"I was upstairs in bed."

"What else did you hear?"

"I heard him walking in the kitchen downstairs. Then I heard three shots and Father falling to the floor."

"Where was your mother?"

"She was in her bedroom upstairs."

"What did you do?"

"Mother and the rest of us went downstairs and found Father on the floor."

"Was he alive?"

"Not much."

"Then what happened?"

"We tried calling the sheriff, but the phone didn't work."

"What did you do then?"

"We went back to bed, and the next morning, Mother told me to run to Olson's place to call the sheriff."

"When did the sheriff get to your home?"

"It was about eight in the morning."

"Some time ago, John left home and went to Redridge to work, is that correct?"

"Yes."

"Why did he do that?"

"Father never bought clothes for him or paid him for what he did. John just wanted to earn some money to buy his own clothes."

"Your father never bought John any clothes?"

"No."

"Did your father ever buy you any clothes?"

"Well, not very much."

"Did John visit with your folks after he moved away?"

"Yes. And he came home to help with the haying."

"Was there any bad feeling between your father and John?"

"No, sir."

Merrill says, "Thank you, Herbert."

Mr. Burritt has no questions.

TESTIMONY OF JOHN EICHKERN

Mr. Merrill calls John Eichkern, the coroner.

Eichkern said Undersheriff Heikkila summoned him to the Lahnala home on Sunday, September 6, 1914. Mr. Eichkern found the deceased, August Lahnala, laying on the kitchen floor. He was wearing shoes, pants, a blue flannel shirt, and underwear. He had a bullet hole with some blood near his right collarbone.

Since this was simply a recitation of facts found at the murder scene, Mr. Burritt has no questions for the defense.

TESTIMONY OF WILLIAM HEIKKILA

Mr. Merrill calls William Heikkila, the undersheriff in 1914. Heikkila says he was called to the Lahnala home on September 6 and he, Sheriff Cruse, and Coroner John Eichkern reached the home about 8 a.m. They noticed the telephone wires were cut at the road, and then they proceeded to the house, where they found Mr. Lahnala laying on the kitchen floor on his back with a bullet wound on his right side. His testimony largely repeated the testimony he provided in the first trial on February 26, 1915.

On cross-examination, Mr. Burritt asks Heikkila, "What caliber was the bullet that killed Mr. Lahnala?"

Heikkila says, "It's a .32-caliber."

Burritt asks, "And you learned afterward that Bill or John Lahnala owned a pistol which would fire a .32-caliber bullet?"

"Yes, sir."

"Who purchased that pistol?"

"We learned that Bill Lahnala purchased the pistol, but John also had access to it."

"Did you determine who sold the pistol to Bill Lahnala?"

"He said he got it from Swift's Hardware in Houghton."

Burritt asks, "Did you determine how many .32-caliber pistols Swift's Hardware has sold in the last five years?"

"No, sir."

"It is a rather common caliber pistol, is it not?"

"It is quite common, yes."

"So, there could be fifty, or a hundred, or several hundred .32-caliber pistols in the county. Is that true?"

"I guess it could be true."

Alex thinks Barney is making some good points for the defense.

TESTIMONY OF WILLIAM LUCAS

Mr. Merrill requests Deputy Sheriff William Lucas to take the stand. Mr. Lucas relates how he and Sheriff Cruse had discussed August's sons, Bill and John, and what they might know about the matter. They agreed that Mr. Lucas should travel to the Rumley area, find out where the boys were the night of the murder, and proceed accordingly.

Lucas says when he was in Marquette, traveling to Rumley shortly after the murder, he overheard a discussion about a man getting shot in Houghton. He asked about the details and learned that the men talking about the shooting were John and Bill Lahnala. Lucas immediately changed his plans and returned to Houghton. As the train traveled to Houghton, he talked with the men some more. Before the train got to Houghton, Lucas had arrested John for the murder.

Mr. Burritt has no questions.

TESTIMONY OF FRED JOHNSON

Mr. Merrill says, "I call Fred Johnson."

After Johnson is sworn and sits in the witness stand, Mr. Merrill asks, "Your name is Fred Johnson?"

"Yes, sir."

"Where do you live?"

"I live on the Canal Road."

"And do you know John Lahnala?"

"Yes, sir."

"And calling your attention to Friday evening, September 4, 1914, where were you?"

"I was in Houghton at Gekas' Candy Kitchen."

"Who was with you?"

"Three girls: Selma Hermanson, Elizabeth Olson, and Hilja Olson."

"I will ask if you saw John Lahnala when you were sitting at your table?"

"I didn't see him until Selma said, 'There is John Lahnala.' I turned my head, and I noticed him there."

"When you were at the Candy Kitchen, did you notice what John was doing?"

"I never noticed anything more than I just saw him standing there when my attention was called, and just then he turned around and walked out."

Under cross-examination, Mr. Burritt gets Mr. Johnson to admit that, at the time of the murder, he hadn't seen John in a long time. Fred also admits that he was preoccupied with the women he was entertaining and not paying much attention to other things. Burritt also asks Mr. Johnson about how positive he is that it was John he saw.

Mr. Johnson said, "I thought it was him, but I can't swear to it."

TESTIMONY OF HILDA SOLMONSON

Miss Hilda Solmonson is next to be called by Mr. Merrill. She testifies that she has known John Lahnala since they were children and that she worked with John at Zurcher's dairy farm. They kept company at times.

Merrill asks, "Did you ever hear John say menacing words about his father?"

She replies, "Once when John and his father weren't getting along, John produced a pistol and said, 'With this I will bore that old slouch through.'" She also confirmed that John sometimes found fault with his father because August beat his mother.

The Defense has no questions.

TESTIMONY OF EINO TORVINEN

Mr. Merrill calls John Lahnala's boyhood friend, Eino Torvinen, to the stand. Eino testifies that he and John Lahnala were hunting in the fall of 1913. While hunting, John complained of his father's treatment. When he was working at Redridge, John was underage. Another worker told him that his father could try to collect John's wages. Eino testifies that John said if the old man attempted to collect his wages, he would shoot him.

Mr. Burritt has no questions for the Defense.

TESTIMONY OF MRS. FRED JOHNSON

Mrs. Fred Johnson, who was Miss Elizabeth Olson but married Mr. Johnson since the first trial, offers a positive identification. On the night of the killing, she testifies she and her sister left their home in West Hancock about twenty minutes before eight o'clock and walked slowly to Houghton, going into Gekas' store for ice cream. While there, she said John Lahnala came in. He was not well dressed. She has known Lahnala since he was a boy and is well acquainted with him and his family, with whom she is related by marriage.

On cross-examination, Mrs. Johnson says she cannot remember when she last saw Lahnala before this particular night. She also cannot remember whether she had turned to look at him in the store or faced him as she sat at a table.

Mr. Burritt asks her if she had not told members of her family that she was not certain that it was John Lahnala she saw in the store. She says she has not said that.

Mr. Burritt asks, "You think it was John Lahnala you saw?"

"I know it was him," she answered.

"But you cannot recall if you were facing him or not! I submit that your memory is rather weak on matters of relative importance!" said Burritt.

The Court says, "That is uncalled for, Mr. Burritt."

"I apologize, Your Honor."

"I have no further questions of this witness."

Prosecuting Attorney Merrill stands to address the Court. He says, "The People rest, Your Honor."

Alex isn't expecting that. Compared to the first trial, the Prosecution hasn't presented many witnesses and hasn't built a very strong case. Alex is thinking maybe it seemed longer and more detailed the first time around because it was all new to him. Or maybe the Prosecution is only presenting a half-hearted case because Mr. Merrill has concluded that John did not get a fair shake during the first trial.

Alex thinks, *Whatever the reason, we'll take it!*

The Daily Mining Gazette

Wednesday, February 28, 1917

PROSECUTION NEARS END OF ITS SIDE OF CASE

Eino Torvinen, Boyhood Friend of Defendant Testifies That in Fall of 1913 Lahnala Threatened to Kill Father - Prosecution Rests Today

It is expected that during today's session of the Lahnala murder trial the prosecution will rest, and that Attorney Burritt will be able to open the case for the defense. Prosecuting Attorney Merrill yesterday expressed this opinion.

The Chain of Evidence

The chain of evidence that the prosecution attempts to complete before it rests today offers the theory that John Lahnala left Rumley, Alger County, on the morning of September 4 and arrived on the night train to Houghton; that this train arrived in Houghton at 8:09 that night, in time for Lahnala to have appeared in the Gekas' Candy Kitchen as testified to by various witnesses. The theory then follows Lahnala to Oskar, the shooting of his father, walking from Oskar to Houghton to catch the train leaving Houghton at 10:55, connecting at 1:15 with a train from Duluth and arriving at Rumley some time that Sunday.

Defense Witnesses Arrive

B. J. Goodman of Marquette, manager of the Little Lake Lumber Company at Little Lake, Marquette County, arrived in Houghton yesterday. He is the principal witness for the defense. At the first trial he gave what the defense claimed to be a perfect alibi for Lahnala.

Conductor Albert St. Cyr, who had charge of a train in the Little Lake vicinity, also arrived yesterday as a witness for the defense. The presumption is that he will testify that he saw Lahnala near Little Lake at about the time Goodman did.

Big Crowds Yesterday

The attendance yesterday was the largest since the trial opened, the afternoon crowd being so large that it filled all the standing room in the place reserved for spectators, after the seats had been taken.

Chapter 38
Witnesses for the Defense

The Court says, "Mr. Burritt, if you are ready to proceed with your arguments, please call your first witness."

Barney says, "Thank you, Your Honor. The Defense calls William Ollie."

TESTIMONY OF WILLIAM OLLIE

Mr. Ollie relates that he saw his brother-in-law, John Lahnala, and John's brother Bill together on September 6, the day after the murder. Ollie testified that John and Bill Lahnala called at his home near Rumley Sunday morning, the day after the killing of John's father. Ollie said it was early in the morning because he had not yet breakfasted.

Burritt is trying to show the jury the importance of time in this situation. If John was in the Copper Country Saturday evening, he could not have gotten back to Rumley at an early hour Sunday.

Mr. Merrill has no questions.

TESTIMONY OF MRS. EVA KURU THROUGH AN INTERPRETER

Mr. Burritt calls Mrs. Eva Kuru and asks, "Did you invite Mrs. Lahnala to your place on the eighteenth of October 1914?"

"Yes."

"What did you want to talk about with Mrs. Lahnala?"

"I wanted to talk about a discussion I had with her late husband, August."

"And what did you share about that discussion?"

"I said I was talking to August before he was killed, and he said he was fearing for his life."

"When you had this discussion with August, how did you react to what he said?"

"I told him that's pretty disturbing."

"Is that all he said?"

"No. He also said he was at the Finnish Hall, and someone gritted his teeth and said he'd kill him if he dared."

"Did he say who said that to him?"

"No."

"What was Mrs. Lahnala's reaction to all of this?"

"All she said was August has definitely changed in the last couple of years and he seems to be rubbing many people the wrong way."

"Was that all she said?"

"No. She also said she wondered who could have said that to him. But that was all."

Burritt says, "Thank you, Mrs. Kuru. Nothing further, Your Honor."

Mr. Merrill has no questions on behalf of the People.

Alex is thinking, "I wonder why Greta was not more concerned? If someone threatened the life of my spouse, I'd be much more concerned! Could it be because she knows August had a long list of enemies, so this wasn't anything new to her? Or is it because she just didn't care anymore, and her life would be easier without August in it?"

TESTIMONY OF JOHN LEHTO

Mr. Burritt calls for Mr. John Lehto and asks, "In 1914, what was your occupation?"

Lehto answers, "I owned a saloon and boarding house in Hancock."

"Did you know August Lahnala?"

"Yes, I did."

"Did Mr. Lahnala ever stay overnight at your boarding house?"

"He asked me to let him stay the night. I said he could, but I'm not sure that he did. I was working in the bar, and another man was taking care of the boarding house."

"Do you recall when that was?"

"It was late summer of 1914."

"Did he say why he wanted to stay at your place?"

"He said someone threatened to kill him, and he was afraid to go home that night."

"Did he say who threatened him?"

"He did not."

"Could you tell if Mr. Lahnala had been drinking that night?"

"I couldn't say he was drunk, but he had been drinking."

Under cross-examination, Mr. Merrill asks, "What time was it that he came to your bar and spoke to you?"

"It was close to eleven o'clock. It was quite late."

"And it was plain to be seen that he had been drinking?"

"Yes, a little, but he didn't appear to be drunk."

TESTIMONY OF WILLIAM HEIKKILA

Mr. Burritt calls William Heikkila, the undersheriff, and asks, "The day after the shooting, you made an examination around the Lahnala house, didn't you?"

"Yes, sir."

"Did you find any places where anyone had been laying down or standing up or any evidence of that kind around the house?"

"Just a short distance from the house, it seemed as though somebody lay in the field there."

"You found someplace out near the oat field where it looked as if somebody had been laying down?"

"Yes, sir."

"Was there any indication of who or what had been laying there?"

"No, sir. We figured it could have been a person or maybe a deer that made it look like that."

"Did you see any deer hoofprints in the ground in that area?"

"No, we didn't."

"So, you thought it could have been a person laying there?"

"Yes, sir."

"If it was a person who lay down there, could that person see somebody approaching the house from the main road?"

Merrill objects, saying, "I object, Your Honor. That calls for speculation by the witness."

The Court rules, "Sustained."

Shifting gears, Burritt asks, "Mr. Heikkila, did you find any tools near the pole where the wires were cut?"

"Yes, sir."

"Please describe what you found."

"We found some pliers at the base of the pole."

"Did you think that they might have been used to cut the telephone wires on the pole?"

"Yes, sir."

"Did you try to determine who owned the pliers?"

"Well, after Lahnala was arrested, we figured they must be his."

"Did you ask him if they are his?"

"Yes, sir. He denied ever seeing them."

"Did you do any further follow-up regarding the ownership of the pliers?"

"I did not. Others may have."

Shifting gears yet again, Burritt asks Heikkila, "You ever hear of a fellow by the name of Jack Lacy?"

"Yes, sir."

"Who was he?"

"I don't know much about him, but I understand that he served time in Ionia State Prison."

"Are you aware that August Lahnala testified in a case against Jack Lacy?"

"Yes, sir."

"Did you look him up, try to get any further information on him?"

"We couldn't find any information about him. So, we let it go."

"Did you know that Lacy spent a long time in prison?"

"Yes."

"Did you think that he might have some bad feelings toward Lahnala?"

"Yes, we thought he might hold a grudge."

"What caused you to stop checking further on him?"

"We couldn't find any recent information on Lacy. It didn't seem like he lived in the area. We didn't know where he was."

"So, you just stopped trying to find any information on him?"

"Yes, sir."

Burritt asks, "Would you be surprised to learn that Lacy died about eight years ago in Detroit?"

"Yes, I would."

"On behalf of our client, the defense team asked some questions and eventually learned that he died in Memorial Hospital on May 19, 1909."

Merrill interjects, "Is there a question for the witness?"

Judge O'Brien glares at Burritt.

Burritt continues, asking, "Do you know the name of Jacob Miller, associated with this case?"

"Yes, sir."

"Where was Jacob Miller living at the time of August's death?"

"He was living close to Oskar, not too far from Lahnala."

"You're aware there was some bad blood between Lahnala and this man, Miller?"

"Yes, sir."

"And what was the basis of that bad blood?"

"I was told that Miller was not satisfied with what Lahnala paid for his horse, which died while in Lahnala's service."

"Did you suspect that Mr. Miller might harbor some hatred toward Lahnala?"

"We didn't give it too much thought."

"Why did you not pursue his trail further?"

Heikkila answers, "I did talk to Miller, but he was not feeling too good. We were advised to not follow up on him right away. There were lots of rumors and speculation. The sheriff put different officers checking different leads and possibilities. We started looking at those other possibilities and started digging into other rumors."

"What prompted you to look at John Lahnala?"

"When he was arrested, we were assigned to get evidence in that direction."

"So, you didn't give Miller too much more thought?"

"That's true."

"And you investigated different sources about getting some indication of their interest in August Lahnala, and they were people who had a grudge, that somebody might have killed him for revenge?"

"It seemed like somebody must have had a grudge."

"You're aware that Miller died at the hospital on December 9, 1914, just three months after the shooting?"

"No, I didn't know that."

"You heard the testimony Mrs. Kuru gave a few minutes ago?"

"Yes."

"And she mentioned somebody threatened August Lahnala in 1914 at the Finnish Hall?"

"Yes."

"Did you check into the whereabouts of Mr. Miller the night of the shindig at the Finnish Hall?"

"No, sir."

"You don't know where Mr. Miller was that evening?"

"No, sir."

Burritt asks, "You heard the testimony offered here by Mr. Ollie?"

"I did."

"And you understand that if the defendant was at Mr. Ollie's home in Little Lake early on Sunday, September 6, he could not have been in Houghton the evening before, September 5?"

Mr. Merrill objects. "Your Honor. This is not proper questioning! What Mr. Heikkila understands is merely speculation and has no bearing on the matter at hand!"

The Court agrees. "Objection sustained. Mr. Burritt, please limit your questions to what the witness saw or did."

Burritt says, "I'm sorry, Your Honor. Thank you, Mr. Heikkila. Your witness, Mr. Merrill."

Mr. Merrill says, "No questions."

"No questions!" Alex says to himself. *"The Defense just showed how inept the investigation was by finding Lacy themselves and by poking holes in the thinking of a law enforcement officer involved in a murder investigation, and 'The People' have no questions? The wholly inadequate investigation is being followed by the Prosecution offering nothing to explain their thinking or reasoning. That's hard to believe!"*

TESTIMONY OF EVERT WALITALO

Mr. Burritt next calls Evert Walitalo. After he is sworn to tell the truth, Mr. Walitalo confirms that he knows sisters Hilja Olson and Elizabeth Olson (now Mrs. Fred Johnson), that he had a discussion with them both a few days after the murder, that they both thought the man they saw in the candy store was John Lahnala, that the man didn't say anything, so they were not sure it was him, and that they couldn't take an oath on it.

Mr. Merrill has no questions.

TESTIMONY OF HILJA OLSON

Mr. Burritt next calls Hilja Olson.

Alex wonders what is going through his sister Hilja's mind right now. In the first trial, Hilja said she saw John at Gekas' under direct examination. Under cross-examination, she admitted to talking to several others, including police officers, and strengthening her belief that it was John she saw. But she then had to admit that she couldn't swear it was him. What will her story be this time around?

Burritt asks Hilja, "Do you know Mrs. Matilda Wayrynen?"

"Yes, sir."

"Have you talked to her frequently about this trial?"

"Yes. We talk about many things."

"Did you tell Mrs. Wayrynen that you weren't sure that it was John you saw in the candy store?"

"I may have. But we have talked about many things in the last year or so."

"The Court interjects, "The witness need not participate in repartee. Please just answer the questions put to you."

"Did you tell her, 'I thought it was him I saw, but I'm not sure. If he had said something, I might have been sure.' Didn't you say something like that to Mrs. Wayrynen?"

"Yes, sir, but I still think that it was him."

"But you told her you weren't sure. You cannot swear it was him. Is that what you said?"

"Yes, sir."

"Thank you, Miss Olson."

Mr. Merrill says, "No questions."

Alex thinks, *Well, I'm glad my sister didn't say anything different than her testimony in the first trial.* Alex is also thinking that the Prosecution is offering a rather ineffective case.

Chapter 39
John Lahnala Testimony

John Lahnala is the next witness to be called by Barney Burritt. He is on the witness stand for more than a full day and repeats his story that he was in Rumley, that he looked for work with his brother Bill, that on Thursday September 3, 1914 he was hired by Mr. Lindeman at the Little Lake train depot, that he did some drinking with Lindeman, and that he spent the night at Lindeman's place.

On Friday, September 4, he testifies that he did some more drinking, that he didn't feel well, that he left Lindeman to go to sleep in a field, that he woke in the dark, that he fell asleep again and slept until morning, that he walked to Goodman's store and purchased a lunch of sardines and crackers at Goodman's store, that he went in the pines near the slab piles at the Goodman mill to eat his lunch, that he took the train and then walked to his brother Bill's place, that he spent the night there, that he went with Bill to Ollie's, that Bill shot a deer, and then he learned of his father's death.

The Daily Mining Gazette

Friday, March 2, 1917

JOHN LAHNALA GOES ON STAND IN OWN DEFENSE

Defendant Tells Story That He Hopes Will Convince Jury He Did Not Kill His Father

The case for the defense opened at the beginning of the morning session and Attorney Burritt first put on witnesses to refute the testimony of witnesses who had testified for the purpose of showing that Lahnala was in Houghton County the day of the murder.

The People offered the evidence of the Misses Olson, who swore they saw Lahnala in a Houghton candy store, the night before the murder. Evert Walitalo testified to the general effect that after the girls had returned from the preliminary examination of Lahnala shortly after his arrest, they had stated at Oskar they were not sure the man they saw in the store was Lahnala.

Mr. Burritt called Hilja Olson to the witness stand, who testified she couldn't swear it was John Lahnala she saw in the candy store the night before the murder.

Lahnala's Story Unchanged

John Lahnala, defendant in the murder trial in progress in the Houghton County circuit court, yesterday morning took the stand in his own defense and told substantially the same story he told at the first trial. He said that he was not quite 17 years of age when his father was killed.

Lahnala withstood yesterday's ordeal well and did not depart in any essential particular from the story he told in the first trial. The crux of this story is that he spent the night sleeping in the woods near Little Lake and in the early afternoon he came into that village and bought food at the store of the lumber company. This is the point on which the defense relies, the presumption being that if Lahnala was at Little Lake in Marquette County early in the afternoon of September 5, 1914, he could not have been in Houghton County about 8 o'clock that same night.

Chapter 40
Threats on August's Life

TESTIMONY OF FRED RINTALA

Burritt next calls for Fred Rintala to take the stand. After the regular oath-taking, Burritt asks, "You live in Oskar?"

"Yes, sir."

"What can you tell us about this case?"

"Well, I know that August Lahnala borrowed a horse from Jake Miller, and the horse died while still in Lahnala's possession."

"And Lahnala paid for the horse?"

"Miller said he paid something, but he still owed more money for the horse."

"How did Miller feel about that?"

"He felt he waited long enough for payment. He said if August didn't pay soon, he'd do something else to get his revenge."

"And where did he make this threat?"

"I was in Schmidt's Bar with Alex Peltonen when he said that."

"When did he make that threat?"

"It was the middle of August 1914."

"And Mr. Peltonen heard that?"

Mr. Merrill objects, "He can't testify as to what somebody else heard. He doesn't know what someone else heard."

The Court agrees and sustains the objection.

"Your witness." says Burritt.

Merrill says, "The People have no questions."

TESTIMONY OF ALEX PELTONEN

Burritt calls for Alex Peltonen and asks, "You were a neighbor of Lahnala?"

"Yes."

"You live pretty close to the Lahnala farm?"

"Yes, sir."

"And you were with Mr. Rintala in Schmidt's Bar as Mr. Rintala just testified?"

"Yes, I was."

"Did you hear Miller threaten August Lahnala, as Rintala just testified?"

"Yes, I did."

Mr. Merrill has no cross-examination.

Chapter 41
Sauna Confession?

TESTIMONY OF AXEL ANTILA

Burritt calls Axel Antila to take the stand. After he is sworn, Burritt asks, "Your name is Axel Antila?"

"It is."

"What is your occupation?"

"I have a public sauna in Dollar Bay."

"You operate a public sauna in Dollar Bay?"

"My wife and I do, yes."

"Did you know Jacob Miller?"

"I did."

"Did he take sauna at your establishment in early December 1914?"

"He did."

"Do you recall the date Miller took the sauna at your place?"

"I don't know the exact date, but it was early in December."

"And did you have any discussion with him?"

"Yes, I did."

"What was the substance of that discussion?"

"He said he wasn't feeling well after he took sauna, and he said he should probably see a doctor. But he said he had a heavier mental burden which was weighing him down."

"Did he say anything else about the mental burden?"

"No, he didn't. He left our place right after he said that."

"And he has since died?"

"Yes. I understand he did."

"Your witness, Mr. Merrill."

"We have no questions," says Merrill.

TESTIMONY OF TOPIAS ANTILA

After she is sworn, Barney Burritt asks, "You are Mrs. Axel Antila?"

"I am."

"You heard the testimony given a few minutes ago by your husband?"

"I did."

"Did you know Jacob Miller?"

"I did."

"Can you confirm that what your husband testified is accurate?"

"I can. I was present when he and Jacob had that discussion."

"Did he say anything else about his mental burden?"

"No, he didn't."

"Thank you, Mrs. Antila."

No questions by the People.

On Saturday, March 3, 1917, *The Daily Mining Gazette* published an exhaustive report on the day's proceedings.

The Daily Mining Gazette

Saturday, March 3, 1917

JOHN LAHNALA FIGHTS BRAVELY FOR LIBERTY

Defendant in Murder Trial Stands Up Well Under the Stiff Cross-Examination

The question of whether John Lahnala, the 20-year-old Oskar boy, murdered his father at Oskar on the night of September 5, 1914, is for the jury to decide. But there is no doubt that the youth has won the sympathy of the large audiences attending the trial.

Prosecuting Attorney Merrill poured a continuous stream of questions at him when he was on the stand and the boy held up under the attack and answered all without visible uneasiness, excepting the hesitation that comes from a limited knowledge of English.

Lahnala had some schooling at Oskar. He began doing farm work when a child and he testified yesterday that pretty generally the people of Oskar spoke Finnish when communicating with one another. Mr. Merrill made it appear that it was almost incredible that the Finnish language should be in such common use at Oskar.

Lahnala testified at the first trial two years ago in Finnish, through an interpreter. He has learned to speak English rather fluently, though with a limited vocabulary, since that time, in Marquette prison. He is a little weak on English idioms. For example, Mr. Merrill asked:

"Did you sleep sound?"

"I don't know what you mean – sound." answered the witness.

Lahnala's Own Story

Lahnala's story in detail would make up a volume but in brief it is as follows:

Beginning at New Swanzy about noon of September 3, he was hired by Section Foreman Lindeman, and he remained with Lindeman 'til noon the next day, Friday, the day before the murder at Oskar. He quit Lindeman at noon.

While in Lindeman's company that two half days they drank considerable beer and whisky. John had a bottle of whisky when he left Lindeman, which was at Little Lake, they having reached there on a track inspection trip. He was sleepy and not feeling well and he lay down a short distance from the track to await the arrival of the train. He fell asleep, missed the train, and did not wake up 'til dark. Then he drank the rest of his whisky and decided to spend the night in the woods.

In the morning he came into Little Lake, had more drinks at a nearby saloon, went back into the woods for another sleep and shortly after noon came to Goodman's store at the Little Lake mill and bought a lunch. In the afternoon he took a train and went to Rumley to the home of his brother Bill. This was on Saturday, the day of the murder. Sunday morning, he and his brother went hunting, getting up about 7 o'clock.

Avoids a Pitfall

Lahnala insists that he was not in Houghton County, after he left for Rumley early in the summer, until he came back to attend his father's funeral. He was not in Gekas' Candy Kitchen. "These people are mistaken, then?" asked Mr. Merrill. "Yes, mistaken or telling a lie." Lahnala replied.

Whenever Mr. Merrill would ask Lahnala a question regarding his coming to Houghton the witness would insist that the prosecutor would say what trip he referred to. If the question appeared to be seeking an admission that he was in Houghton September 4 or 5, Lahnala would reiterate "I was in Marquette County at that time."

Points to Another Slayer

Attorney Burritt introduced a new element into the case yesterday, the possibility that another hand than that of John Lahnala's might have fired the shots that killed Lahnala's father.

Fred Rintala and Alex Peltonen, residents of Oskar and neighbors of Lahnala, testified that sometime before Lahnala's death, Lahnala borrowed a horse from Jacob Miller, a neighbor. While he had possession of the horse, the animal died and Lahnala did not satisfy Miller in regard to the matter. These witnesses testified that Miller threatened Lahnala's life.

Topias and Axel Antila, owners of a Finnish massage and bathhouse at Dollar Bay testified that Jacob Miller was in their bathhouse sometime after Lahnala's death. He complained of being ill but also of a mental load that was more painful. He did not state what the weight on his mind was. He went from Dollar Bay to a hospital and died there a few days later.

Corroborative Testimony

Bill Lahnala and his wife, brother, and sister-in-law of John, have testified that John came home to Rumley from Little Lake that Saturday night, slept in their house, and got up and went hunting with Bill Sunday morning. They corroborate John's testimony about his whereabouts on Saturday night, the night of the murder of his father.

Chapter 42
Southern U. P. Witnesses

Mr. Burritt then presents several of the strongest witnesses for the defense.

TESTIMONY OF JOSEPH ROBARGE

After confirming that Joseph Robarge was clerking in Goodman's store on September 5, 1914, Barney asks if he's ever seen John Lahnala before.

"I saw him at the store about two years ago," Robarge replies.

Barney asks, "When was it you think you saw him there?"

"The early part of September."

"Do you remember the exact day?"

"I think it was on the fifth of September."

"About what time of day?"

"In the afternoon. It was around two o'clock."

"Did you transact any business with him?"

"I sold him a can of sardines and a package of crackers."

"And where was Mr. Goodman when this boy came in the store?"

"He and I was standing near the counter, talking. When this gentleman came in, Mr. Goodman made a remark that the man was coming in to bum a lunch or something to that effect. Mr. Goodman stepped outside the counter, the man paid for what he wanted, and we started talking again."

"Was anything then said by Mr. Goodman that causes you to remember the circumstances of this boy coming in?"

"After the man went out, Mr. Goodman said he was surprised because he thought he was going to bum a lunch from me."

"What fixes the date of September 5 in your mind?"

"Well, when you, Mr. Burritt, were in the store asking questions in September 1914, you mentioned the date of September 5 and caused it to stick in my head."

"In 1914, when I asked you about him coming to the store, you told me that you remembered him, didn't you?"

"No, sir."

"When I showed you his photograph, why did you say no when I asked if you had seen him?"

"Well, at the time I didn't feel as though I wanted to get mixed up in the affair. When I found out what was going on, I didn't want to get mixed up in it whatsoever."

"And why should we believe that what you're saying today is the truth?"

"I was subpoenaed and have taken an oath. I feel I must testify truthfully."

"When was the next time you saw this boy after the date you saw him in the store in 1914?"

"Not until this morning."

"Did you recognize him?"

"Yes, sir."

"Would the fact that you are in the employ of the Little Lake Lumber Company and the further fact that Mr. Goodman, your boss, is here as a witness, influence you in any way in giving testimony here on this trial?"

"No, sir."

"You are sure the defendant is the man you saw in the store on

September 5, 1914?"

"Yes, I am."

Mr. Merrill has no questions on behalf of the People.

TESTIMONY OF BERNARD GOODMAN

Mr. Burritt calls for Mr. Bernard J. Goodman.

Barney Burritt says, "You are Bernard J. Goodman?"

"I am."

"Will you tell us, please, what line of work you're in?"

"I am vice president and general manager of the Little Lake Lumber Company."

Burritt asks, "Did you ever see this defendant, John Lahnala, before?"

"Yes, I saw him twice before."

"Please tell us where you've seen him."

With a well-modulated voice, Goodman says, "I saw him at our store in Little Lake and in Houghton at the first trial."

"Can you confirm that you saw John Lahnala at your store in Little Lake on Saturday, September 5, 1914?"

"I can confirm that I saw him on that date."

"How are you so certain you saw this man?"

"I saw this man come into the store, and I thought he is poor and would ask for a handout. But he purchased the crackers and sardines from our clerk, Mr. Robarge. That stood out in my mind."

"And there is no doubt in your mind that the defendant is the man you saw that day?"

"None whatsoever."

"Thank you, Mr. Goodman."

Mr. Merrill says he has no questions, and the Court says, "You may step down, Mr. Goodman."

Judge O'Brien announces, "Well, we've made considerable progress today, so I think we'll adjourn for the day. Court will reconvene on Monday, March 5, at 10:00 a.m."

In the Sunday issue of the local newspaper, the following article appeared.

The Daily Mining Gazette
Sunday, March 4, 1917

LAHNALA TRIAL ATTRACTS MANY

Attendance Increases

The attendance at the John Lahnala trial yesterday was larger than even the preceding two days when the public interest in the trial seemed to have reached its zenith. The regular and extra seating was occupied, and the aisles were filled with standing spectators. A large number of the spectators were public school pupils, apparently sent to take notes on the trial. Women continue to comprise a large proportion of the attending crowd.

It was not possible yesterday to arrive at the approximate time the case would go to the jury. Mr. Burritt has not yet closed for the defense and will put in testimony again tomorrow. The prosecution will have rebuttal testimony, and it would not astonish the court officials if the case consumed the greater part of this week, though a verdict surely is expected before Saturday.

When court reconvenes on March 5, Barney Burritt calls Howard St. John to take the stand.

TESTIMONY OF HOWARD ST. JOHN

Burritt begins by asking, "What is your name and occupation?"

"I am Howard St. John. I am auditor as well as the general freight and passenger agent of the Marquette, Munising, and Southeastern Railroad."

"Will you briefly explain how your auditing function pertains to this case?"

"I'll try. For either the entire journey of a train, or for each leg of a train's journey, a passenger needs a ticket. A passenger can either pay at the station for his entire journey prior to boarding the train or, if he hasn't purchased a ticket at the station, he can pay the conductor after he is on the train. The conductor records in his book whatever fares are paid directly to him. At the end of the day, I tally the cash from the conductor and ensure it matches the conductor's report of the number of passengers aboard the train."

"What does your audit show for the afternoon of September 5, 1914?"

"It shows that Mr. St. Cyr, the conductor, sold a single ticket for travel from Little Lake to Lawson on the afternoon of September 5 and the same from Lawson to Rumley."

"Thank you, Mr. St. John."

Mr. Merrill has no questions.

TESTIMONY OF ALBERT ST. CYR

Burritt says, "I call Albert St. Cyr."

After Mr. St. Cyr takes the stand and the oath, Burritt asks him, "How are you involved in this case?"

St. Cyr says, "I called the Burritt & Burritt law firm on March 18, 1915, after the first trial ended. I am a conductor on the Marquette, Munising, and Southeastern Railroad and can vouch for John Lahnala being on the train near Rumley the afternoon of September 5, 1914."

"Why does that date stand out in your mind?"

"I recall a young man on the train who didn't have a ticket. I collected a cash fare from him. The man seemed unusually sensitive when I reprimanded him for not having a ticket. It was the only cash fare I collected that day."

Burritt asks, "Did you also testify to these events at the first trial, which ended in March 1915?"

"I did not."

"Why were you silent then?"

"I didn't testify at the first trial because I didn't hear about the trial until I heard of John Lahnala's conviction. I also heard that a deputy was in the Rumley area, looking for information about a young Finn, but I didn't think that the Finn could be the man who rode on my train."

"What prompted you to get involved now?"

"I heard more details of the case, so I looked at my train receipts and confirmed that there was only one cash fare slip on September 5. I took it upon myself to go to the Marquette Branch Prison to identify Lahnala, and I recognized him immediately in the prison yard."

"And you are sure this man is the one who rode the train?"

"I am positive Lahnala is the man who rode the train and who I reprimanded on September 5, 1914."

"Thank you, Mr. St. Cyr." says Burritt.

Mr. Merrill has no questions on behalf of the People.

TESTIMONY OF PHILLIP HOFFMAN

Mr. Burritt says, "Please state your name and occupation."

"My name is Philip Hoffman, and I cook in the woods and do other work in Mr. Goodman's mill."

"Where were you working on Saturday, the fifth of September 1914?"

"I was working on the whitewash machine at the mill."

"Was the whitewash machine working?"

"Well, it worked but it was leaking, and it needed repairs."

"And who else was working with you?"

"Paul Johnson, and there were a couple of other guys in the mill who were also working that day."

"And who told you to whitewash the mill?"

"Mr. Goodman."

"Now, how do you know it was September 5 when you worked whitewashing the mill?"

"I got a book, and I write down everything I do: what I buy, where I work, and much of that kind of detail."

"Have you been asked to do that by Mr. Goodman or others?"

"No, sir. But I've been involved in some mistakes over the years. I decided to protect myself by keeping track of what I do."

"Your witness, Mr. Merrill."

Merrill replies, "I have no questions of this witness."

TESTIMONY OF PAUL JOHNSON

Mr. Burritt next calls Paul Johnson to the stand. Mr. Johnson relates how he works at the Goodman Mill in Little Lake. The mill was not running on September 5, 1914, and he was working on the broken whitewash machine with Phillip Hoffman. While at the mill, he saw a man walking from the store, and he passed by about twenty-five or thirty feet away from Johnson and went into the jack pines. He testifies that John Lahnala was that man, and he cannot be mistaken.

Mr. Merrill says he has no questions.

Mr. Burritt says, "The Defense rests, Your Honor."

Judge O'Brien declares, "At this time, we will take a sixty-minute recess." He pounds his gavel as the people in the courtroom stand.

Almost all of those in the courtroom stay standing to stretch their legs. Some head to the restroom, but most stay near their seats so they don't lose their vantage points. Although court is adjourned, Alex is thinking that the occupants of the room are unusually quiet. There is a murmuring undertone, but he is reading the air of expectancy as a positive sign.

Chapter 43
Closing Arguments

When court reconvenes, the Court asks, "Are you prepared to present your closing argument, Mr. Burritt?"

Barney responds, "I am, Your Honor."

The Court says, "Please proceed."

DEFENSE CLOSING ARGUMENT

Barney Burritt takes nearly three hours to cover each significant point the Defense has made, in hopes of satisfying the jury of John Lahnala's innocence. He presents a factual summary of the case, as well as statements of witnesses who testified that they heard threats made against the victim. His final statements are a summary of his closing argument.

He addresses the jury. "Gentlemen, the case of the Prosecution is based solely on circumstantial evidence. To find a defendant guilty based on circumstantial evidence, the evidence must be inconsistent with all other possible scenarios. If there is another hypothesis which might explain what happened, it is your duty to find the defendant not guilty. The Court will explain this further when it gives you instructions.

"When we started this trial, I said to you that this case is really very simple. You have heard the testimony of witnesses who took an oath to testify truthfully. And they did.

"Witnesses have testified that it would not be possible to be in southern Marquette County, to take the train to Houghton County, to commit the murder, and to return to Marquette County by train, and also to be seen in Houghton at the times testified by some witnesses. It's not possible.

"In addition, we have presented the testimony of several people who have sworn that they saw, or were with, the defendant in southern

Marquette County around the time this murder was committed. We have offered proof that this defendant could not and did not commit this crime.

"We have also presented the testimony of witnesses who heard others make specific threats against the life of the defendant's father, August Lahnala.

"So, it really is that simple, gentlemen. This defendant was in Marquette County when this crime was committed. And I ask you to return a verdict of not guilty against this defendant.

"Thank you."

PROSECUTION CLOSING ARGUMENT

Judge O'Brien asks, "Mr. Merrill, is the Prosecution ready with its closing argument?"

"We are, Your Honor."

"Please proceed."

Mr. Merrill expounds for nearly ninety minutes on his closing argument. As an experienced attorney, Mr. Merrill has had considerable exposure to other legal professionals who can drone on for extended periods of time, enjoy their own oratory, but not say much. And Mr. Merrill shows he learned well from them. His ninety minutes is noteworthy because of what his story didn't prove.

In summary, he says, "Gentlemen of the jury, the Defense appears to have built an imposing wall to protect this defendant from being found guilty of this crime. I only ask you to consider that there have been many dates, and many times, presented in this case. And this crime was committed thirty months ago. That's two-and-a-half years ago. Two-and-a-half years is a long time. I ask you if there is a possibility that memories may have slipped, or details been forgotten, which might have been reflected in testimony which you have heard here.

"Nobody witnessed the murder when it was committed. Therefore, we are left with only circumstantial evidence to make our case: that John Lahnala, this defendant, did willfully murder his father.

"We have presented testimony which shows that this defendant had a deep-seated hatred toward his father. Several witnesses testified that he threatened to kill his father because he would not provide the barest of necessities for his own son: clothes!

"The testimony of the People's witnesses tends to show that this defendant was in Houghton County the evening before the murder was committed. Certainly, we cannot show every footstep which he might have taken at that time. But he is a clever young man and knows this area well. It should not surprise you that he was not often seen as he traveled about.

"We ask that you find this defendant guilty of the premeditated murder of his father.

"Thank you, gentlemen."

Chapter 44
Court's Final Instructions

Since the jury has heard the closing arguments for the Defense and the Prosecution, Judge O'Brien delivers his final instructions to the jury.

"The burden is upon the People to show that the defendant did the killing, that it was done unjustifiably, with deliberation and premeditation, and of his malice aforethought.

"The defendant, gentlemen, is not obliged to prove his innocence. Everyone charged with crime is presumed to be innocent until the contrary is shown beyond a reasonable doubt. Therefore, when this trial commenced, the law presumed the defendant to be innocent of the crime charged against him, and this presumption of innocence attended the defendant at every successive step throughout this trial. Unless and until such presumption of innocence is overcome by evidence which shall convince the jury of the guilt of the defendant beyond all reasonable doubt, it is your duty to acquit him.

"A reasonable doubt is a fair doubt based upon reason and common sense. It is such a doubt where you cannot say you have a moral certainty of the truth of the charge made against the defendant.

"It is the duty of every individual juror to consider the testimony and discuss it with his fellow jurors. If he has a reasonable doubt as to the guilt of the defendant, he should not convict him. On the other hand, if any juror or jurors are convinced of the defendant's guilt beyond a reasonable doubt, such juror or jurors should not consent to a verdict of acquittal.

"He is charged with murdering his father, and the People come into this court seeking to make a case based on circumstantial evidence. Every syllable of it is circumstantial. You have heard a definition of circumstantial evidence and how every link of evidence in the chain of evidence must point to the guilt of the defendant. If any of you have a reasonable doubt, if any of the evidence doesn't point toward his guilt, you must find the defendant innocent of this crime. That's the law.

"Now, gentlemen, you recognize fully that you have a serious and important duty to perform. Weigh the evidence carefully. Consider all the facts and circumstances. If you are convinced beyond a reasonable doubt that this defendant is guilty, you will fearlessly bring in a verdict of guilty of murder in the first degree. On the other hand, if you are not convinced, you should equally as fearlessly bring in a verdict of not guilty. Thank you."

On March 7, 1917, the case was given to the jury.

The Daily Mining Gazette

Thursday, March 8, 1917

LAHNALA JURY HAS NOT YET REPORTED VERDICT

Fate of Young Oskar Farm Youth Is in the Hands of Twelve Men

The Lahnala murder case was given to the jury at 4:45 yesterday afternoon. At 10 o'clock last night Judge O'Brien was notified by Bailiff Trudell that no report had been made by the jury and the judge ordered the twelve to be locked up for the night so that a verdict may not now be expected at least 'til court opens this morning at 9:15. The presumption is that Judge O'Brien will refuse to accept a disagreement from this jury 'til the last hope of an agreement has been dispelled because the case has cost Houghton County, for the second time, a large amount of money.

It was estimated last night that the case will cost the county, when all the bills are paid, not less than $5,000. The first trial probably cost an equal amount.

Big Crowd Is Faithful

The closing hours of the Lahnala trial, which completed its second week, saw just as big an attendance as has been characteristic of the sessions since about the third day. Before Court opened yesterday morning, every seat was occupied and soon the aisles began to be filled with those satisfied with standing room only.

Throughout the trial a considerable number of women have been faithful attendants at every session. Many were only occasional visitors but there were several who never missed a session. This is unusual in Houghton County. This case on its first trial did not attract anything near like the attention it has attracted this time. It is not recalled that in the past 15 years any trial drew such crowds and there have been some celebrated cases in the county in that period.

The Closing Arguments

Attorney Burritt for the defense made a memorable argument on behalf of his client. He relied almost entirely upon the alibi built up on the testimony of the Marquette County witnesses, who saw Lahnala at Little Lake the day of the murder.

Mr. Merrill closed the arguments yesterday afternoon. He proved as adroit in argument as in examination and kept the crowd up to a keen pitch of interest.

Chapter 45
The Verdict

On Thursday, March 8, 1917, Alex and Hilda get to the courtroom early. Although the room is nearly half full when they arrive, there is an eerie quiet about it. There is a hush of subdued voices, but nobody is speaking loudly. Alex compares it to the quiet, respectful time prior to the start of services in his church, when people are doing introspective speculation.

Judge O'Brien convenes the court at 9:30 a.m. The courtroom is extremely crowded. After calling the court to be in session, he asks for more temporary seating to be made available for spectators. More chairs are brought into the room and, after about ten minutes, he calls for order in the court. As in the first trial, Judge O'Brien cautions those in the courtroom to remain calm when the verdict is announced. He asks the jury foreman, "Have you reached a verdict?"

The foreman replies, "We have, Your Honor."

"And what is your verdict?"

"We the jury find the defendant not guilty …" and the rest of his statement is drowned out by the cheering of those in the courtroom.

Judge O'Brien pounds his gavel and shouts, "Order! Order in the court!" Nobody is listening to him. He makes eye contact with the bailiff, and they both smile and shrug their shoulders. He leans back in his chair to enjoy the show.

Alex and John both jump to their feet and hug over the railing that separates them. John hugs his sister Hilda, who is openly weeping for joy. Handshakes and hugs are warm and open among Barney, John, Alex, Hilda, and many others on the defense team and with John's supporters.

Over the din, Barney shouts in Alex's ear, "Dinner is on me at the Douglas House tonight! Of course, Hilda, Greta, and John are also invited. I may not be able to talk to them, so please let them know."

Alex promises, "I will! Thank you!"

After several minutes, Judge O'Brien called for a one-hour court recess. When he again calls the court to order, O'Brien thanks the jury for their attention during the trial and their verdict. He then dismisses John and the jury and recesses court.

The following day, the newspaper carried this story.

The Daily Mining Gazette

Friday, March 9, 1917

JURY FREES LAHNALA OF CHARGE OF PATRICIDE

Oskar Youth is Liberated

Two Years to the Day from the Time He Was Sentenced for Life

Public Sentiment Had Stayed with Him

John Lahnala, charged with the murder of his father, was acquitted by the jury in the Houghton County circuit court yesterday morning. He was given his freedom two years to the day from the time he was sentenced to life in Marquette prison on conviction of the same crime.

The case went to the jury at 4:45 Wednesday afternoon and the verdict was declared at 9:45 yesterday morning.

As soon as the verdict was announced the tension under which the faithful attendants at court had been relaxed and nearly every woman in the room began to sob. The jurymen were affected themselves and tears rolled down the faces of many. Even Bailiff Trudell choked up with emotion and had not recovered sufficiently a few minutes later when the Court told him to announce a recess. Lahnala jumped to his feet when the verdict was announced and shook hands with his attorney, B. H. T. Burritt of Hancock. As soon as he could reach the jury, he shook hands with every man and thanked them.

Public Sentiment Revealed

The instant recess was declared, women in the court room ran up to Lahnala to shake his hand and congratulate him, all expressing the sympathy they had felt for him throughout the trial. It was almost a tangible thing at every session and, if there is anything in telepathy, the jury could not help but feel the urge toward mercy that was being radiated from the attending crowd.

Judge O'Brien formally discharged the defendant after the verdict was announced. Lahnala walked to the bench and said goodbye to the Court and Judge O'Brien advised, "You be a good boy and go home and take care of yourself and your mother."

Lahnala said before leaving the courtroom he planned to go home to Oskar with his widowed mother and his brother and sisters and that he expects to get work in a lumber camp for the winter after a short rest at home. He intends, however, to make his home with his mother and help her work the farm, being now the oldest unmarried member of the family.

Great Victory for Burritt

All concerned in the case concede that the acquittal is a great victory for Attorney B. H. T. Burritt, it being the first big case he has handled unaided. He was the law partner of his father, William A. Burritt, who had conducted the first trial for the defense and who secured this trial from the Michigan Supreme Court. The older Mr. Burritt died shortly before the new trial was granted and his son undertook the defense alone. Mr. Burritt was determined to justify his father's confidence in Lahnala's innocence, and he put a lot of work into his preparations.

Throughout the trial, it has been admitted that both Prosecuting Attorney Merrill and Mr. Burritt had tried the case in a flawless manner. The reputation of each is enhanced by it.

Epilogue

The murder of August Lahnala remains unsolved.

Jacob Miller died in Hancock three months after the murder. This was before the first trial. It's unfortunate that an extensive interview with Mr. Miller was not conducted prior to his death. This could have been done by the law enforcement officials or by the prosecution or defense legal teams.

It is also unfortunate that there was no detailed investigation of evidence introduced in the trials relating to the whereabouts of Mr. Miller when the murder occurred, or during the shindig at the Finnish Hall when August's life was threatened.

John Lahnala eventually married. He moved from the immediate area and had several children.

About the author

Duane (Dewey) Olson is a fourth-generation Finnish-American "Yooper" (person from Michigan's Upper Peninsula, or UP). Alex Olson was his grandfather. August Lahnala, the victim in this story, was his great-grandfather.

Dewey lived the first two years of his life just north of Oskar, where his parents owned and operated a dairy farm. This is the same farm and farmhouse where, thirty-five years earlier, August Lahnala lived. And died.

Due to farming-related injury, his parents found it necessary to sell the farm. The family moved to Hancock where Dewey spent the next twenty years of his life.

www.ingramcontent.com/pod-product-compliance
Lightning Source LLC
LaVergne TN
LVHW052310200926
848481LV00002B/517